Pearl Harbor

Other books in the History Firsthand series:

The Civil War: The North
The Civil War: The South
The Constitutional Convention
Early Black Reformers
The Gold Rush
The Great Depression
The Holocaust: Death Camps
Japanese American Internment Camps
Making and Using the Atomic Bomb
The Middle Ages
The Nuremberg Trial
Pioneers
Prohibition
The Renaissance
The Roaring Twenties
Sixties Counterculture
Slavery
The Vietnam War
War-Torn Bosnia
Women's Suffrage
The World Trade Center Attack

HISTORY
FIRSTHAND

Pearl Harbor

YA
940.54
Pearl

Don Nardo, *Book Editor*

Daniel Leone, *President*
Bonnie Szumski, *Publisher*
Scott Barbour, *Managing Editor*
David M. Haugen, *Series Editor*

GREENHAVEN
PRESS®

THOMSON
———＊———™
GALE

San Diego • Detroit • New York • San Francisco • Cleveland
New Haven, Conn. • Waterville, Maine • London • Munich

LIBRARY OF CONGRESS CATALOGING-IN-PUBLICATION DATA

Pearl Harbor / Don Nardo, book editor.
   p. cm. — (History firsthand)
Includes bibliographical references and index.
ISBN 0-7377-1435-2 (lib. : alk. paper) — ISBN 0-7377-1436-0 (pbk. : alk. paper)
  1. Pearl Harbor (Hawaii), attack on, 1941. 2. World War, 1939–1945—Causes.
3. United States—Foreign relations—Japan. 4. Japan—Foreign relations—United States. 5. Military intelligence—United States—History—20th century. I. Nardo, Don, 1947– . II. Series.
D767.92 .P37 2003
940.54'26—dc21
                                      2002032210

Printed in the United States of America

Contents

Foreword   11

Introduction: December 7, 1941: The Day of Infamy   13

Chapter 1: Prologue to Infamy

Chapter Preface   34

1. Advocating a Strategy of Ambush
by Isoroku Yamamoto   36
Admiral Isoroku Yamamoto, leader of the Japanese
navy's Combined Fleet, strongly advocated the general strategy of a surprise attack on the U.S. Pacific
fleet. Such a plan was adopted and carried out by
Japan on December 7, 1941.

2. Planning the Attack
by Minoru Genda   41
Deciding to launch a surprise attack on Hawaii was
one thing, but making such a huge and bold operation
a reality was quite another. Japanese leaders put air
ace Minoru Genda in charge of planning the assault
and training the pilots.

3. A Fateful Warning Ignored
by Peter J. Shepherd   50
Just three days before the Japanese raid on Pearl Harbor, a British air force technician on a mission in Indochina heard about and reported the impending attack. His warning, however, was ignored.

4. A Suspicious Telephone Call
by Mrs. Motokazu Mori and a Tokyo Newspaper   60
Only two days before Pearl Harbor was bombed, a
dentist's wife in Honolulu, Hawaii, received a call
from Tokyo asking for information about the American fleet. The FBI recorded the call, but the military
took no interest in its suspicious nature.

5. Last-Minute Messages Fail to Avert War
by Franklin D. Roosevelt and the Japanese Government   64
On December 6, 1941, only a few hours before the attack on Pearl Harbor commenced, the American and

Japanese governments exchanged lists of grievances. By this time, however, war was inevitable.

6. Closing In on the Target
by Mitsuo Fuchida   76
The lead pilot of the Japanese attack squadron describes how the secret fleet crossed the Pacific to Hawaii, how the warplanes made their way to Oahu, and how the famous attack began.

Chapter 2: Attack on Battleship Row

Chapter Preface   81

1. The Whistle of Falling Bombs
by Edwin T. Layton   82
The chief intelligence officer of the U.S. Pacific fleet, who was living on Oahu on December 7, 1941, provides a riveting overview of the major events of the attack on Battleship Row.

2. Inside the Danger Zone
by Joseph Ryan   89
From his vantage aboard a rescue craft, young Joseph Ryan saw the Japanese planes cripple one large warship after another, including the *Oklahoma* and *Nevada*.

3. The View from the *Arizona*'s Crow's Nest
by Vernon Olsen   93
While manning his station in the crow's nest of the USS *Arizona*, mechanical difficulties kept Vernon Olsen from firing back at the enemy planes. But he had a sweeping view of the destructive attack on his ship.

4. Abandoning the *Arizona*
by Carl Carson   97
Carl Carson was standing on the deck of the doomed *Arizona* when the huge, fatal explosion occurred. Badly wounded and passing in and out of consciousness, he, along with the other survivors, was forced to abandon ship.

5. Chaos Below Decks
by John H. McGoran   100
In the mazelike compartments below the decks of the mighty USS *California*, stunned sailors felt the war-

ship rise into the air after being struck by a bomb. Then the survivors struggled to aid the wounded and dying.

6. Fire on the Waters
by Bill Steedly   107
Many sailors in Battleship Row were either blown off the decks of their ships or forced to abandon them. Either way, many who made it into the water were killed or injured in the fires that raged on the surface.

7. Caught in the Second Wave of Attackers
by Ephraim P. Holmes   110
A number of U.S. servicemen were far from the harbor and missed the first wave of attackers, only to reach the scene and be caught in the second wave. Lieutenant Ephraim P. Holmes witnessed the second attack from the USS *Maryland*.

Chapter 3: Land Targets and Installations

Chapter Preface   114

1. The Devastation at Hickam Field
by Ginger, a High School Senior   116
Ginger, a seventeen-year-old who lived at Hickam Field, witnessed the assault on the base, nearly losing her life as bombs exploded around her.

2. A Hickam Airman Runs for His Life
by Joseph A. Pesek   120
While Hickam Field was under attack, Sgt. Joseph A. Pesek ran across much of the base, attempting simultaneously to fight back, help his comrades, and stay alive in a deadly rain of bombs and bullets.

3. Assaults on Living Quarters
by Stephen and Flora Belle Koran   125
Ships, docks, airplanes, hangers, trucks, and other military elements were not the only targets of the Japanese warplanes. They also strafed living quarters, as revealed by the narrow escape of an airman and his family.

4. The Fight to Save the Injured
by Ruth Erickson   133
A navy nurse stationed south of Pearl Harbor braved a rain of shrapnel to make it to the hospital and begin

caring for a flood of wounded sailors and other military personnel.

5. Defending the Beaches
by Roy Blick   137
In addition to the main harbor and the airfields, several coastal defense installations on Oahu witnessed or felt the effect of the Japanese attack, including Fort Kamehameha on the island's southern coast.

Chapter 4: The Immediate Aftermath

Chapter Preface   142

1. Escape from the Capsized *Oklahoma*
by Stephen B. Young   144
Though the raid was over, the horror continued for many American sailors trapped in sinking or capsized ships. Some endured many hours of misery and fear as rescue workers raced to free them.

2. The Verbal and Official War Declarations
by Franklin D. Roosevelt and the U.S. Senate   152
On December 8, 1941, President Roosevelt delivered his stirring war declaration against Japan to a joint session of Congress. A few minutes later, the Senate passed it, making it official.

3. Shipping the Wounded Home
by Revella Guest   156
Tripler Army Hospital received what seemed like an endless stream of wounded servicemen following the attack. An army nurse tells how she and her colleagues saved lives and prepared the injured for their journeys home.

4. Salvaging Damaged Ships
by Homer N. Wallin   161
Almost all of the U.S. warships damaged in the Japanese attack were eventually refloated, including the ill-fated *Oklahoma.* The righting of the ships was a tribute to American industrial might, technical skill, and resourcefulness.

5. Congress's Investigation of the Attack
by the U.S. Congress   171
After the end of the war, a congressional committee
looked into the Pearl Harbor incident to determine
how it happened and who was at fault. The conclusion was that Japan was solely responsible for the
disaster.

Chronology   178
For Further Research   181
Index   184
About the Editor   188

Foreword

In his preface to a book on the events leading to the Civil War, Stephen B. Oates, the historian and biographer of Abraham Lincoln, John Brown, and other noteworthy American historical figures, explained the difficulty of writing history in the traditional third-person voice of the biographer and historian. "The trouble, I realized, was the detached third-person voice," wrote Oates. "It seemed to wring all the life out of my characters and the antebellum era." Indeed, how can a historian, even one as prominent as Oates, compete with the eloquent voices of Daniel Webster, Abraham Lincoln, Harriet Beecher Stowe, Frederick Douglass, and Robert E. Lee?

Oates's comment notwithstanding, every student of history, professional and amateur alike, can name a score of excellent accounts written in the traditional third-person voice of the historian that bring to life an event or an era and the people who lived through it. In *Battle Cry of Freedom*, James M. McPherson vividly re-creates the American Civil War. Barbara Tuchman's *The Guns of August* captures in sharp detail the tensions in Europe that led to the outbreak of World War I. Taylor Branch's *Parting the Waters* provides a detailed and dramatic account of the American Civil Rights Movement. The study of history would be impossible without such guiding texts.

Nonetheless, Oates's comment makes a compelling point. Often the most convincing tellers of history are those who lived through the event, the eyewitnesses who recorded their firsthand experiences in autobiographies, speeches, memoirs, journals, and letters. The Greenhaven Press History Firsthand series presents history through the words of first-person narrators. Each text in this series captures a significant historical era or event—the American Civil War, the

Great Depression, the Holocaust, the Roaring Twenties, the 1960s, the Vietnam War. Readers will investigate these historical eras and events by examining primary-source documents, authored by chroniclers both famous and little known. The texts in the History Firsthand series comprise the celebrated and familiar words of the presidents, generals, and famous men and women of letters who recorded their impressions for posterity, as well as the statements of the ordinary people who struggled to understand the storm of events around them—the foot soldiers who fought the great battles and their loved ones back home, the men and women who waited on the breadlines, the college students who marched in protest.

The texts in this series are particularly suited to students beginning serious historical study. By examining these firsthand documents, novice historians can begin to form their own insights and conclusions about the historical era or event under investigation. To aid the student in that process, the texts in the History Firsthand series include introductions that provide an overview of the era or event, timelines, and bibliographies that point the serious student toward key historical works for further study.

The study of history commences with an examination of words—the testimony of witnesses who lived through an era or event and left for future generations the task of making sense of their accounts. The Greenhaven Press History Firsthand series invites the beginner historian to commence the process of historical investigation by focusing on the words of those individuals who made history by living through it and recording their experiences firsthand.

Introduction: December 7, 1941: The Day of Infamy

Now and then events occur that can be called great turning points or watersheds in history—moments when the world changes and political and cultural currents suddenly halt in their tracks and begin moving in unexpected directions. Columbus's 1492 voyage to the New World, the defeat of the Spanish Armada in 1588, the establishment of the United States in 1776, and the terrorist attacks on New York and Washington in September 2001 readily come to mind. The Japanese sneak attack on the U.S. fleet at Pearl Harbor on December 7, 1941, easily ranks with these epic events in its audacity and impact on subsequent world affairs. In particular, Pearl Harbor drew the United States into a world war; this required it suddenly to begin exploiting its enormous industrial and military potential, which in turn rapidly transformed the face of world politics. In the words of historian H.P. Willmott,

> It was a moment when, in the midst of what seemed a disastrous defeat, the United States of America was forced to assume the responsibilities of power and began to tread the road that, very shortly, was to lead her into her inheritance as the greatest power in the world. . . . The United States, through a process that included both defeats and victories, emerged as the world's greatest naval and air power, possessed of unrivalled atomic capacity, and vested with something like three-quarters of the world's industrial output by 1945.[1]

A Long-Standing Contempt for America

If the United States is a superpower today in no small degree because of the attack on Pearl Harbor and the events it spawned, the Japanese certainly did not foresee this develop-

13

ment when they were planning the operation in the summer and fall of 1941. In their view, the United States was only one of several industrial powers in the world (the others were Britain, France, Germany, Italy, the Soviet Union, Australia, and Japan itself). When Japan began its own bold bid for global power in the 1930s, it realized that it would likely need to confront and defeat at least some of these nations.

In particular, most Japanese leaders believed, a war with the United States was inevitable. Indeed, the attack on Pearl Harbor was not an isolated or spontaneous event but, rather, the end result of many years of pent-up Japanese frustration with and contempt for the Americans. Four generations of Japanese had lived with the memory of the humiliation their country had suffered in 1853. At that time, Japan was still a feudal society largely isolated from the rest of the world, and all attempts by British, Russian, and other Western agents to establish relations with Japanese leaders had met with resistance. To overcome this resistance, the United States finally resorted to force. Commodore Matthew Perry sailed a large squadron of American warships to Japan and demanded that the Japanese sign a treaty with the United States. The Japanese said they were not interested. But Perry made it clear that if they did not sign, some kind of violent action would ensue. Intimidated, Japanese leaders reluctantly signed the treaty in 1854, agreeing to allow American ships to resupply in Japanese ports. Seeing the opportunity to exploit Japanese markets, Britain and other nations immediately established trade relations with the Japanese, who now felt they had no other choice but to cooperate.

However, Japan's leaders also felt they must do whatever was necessary to avoid such weakness and subservience to foreigners in the future. They concluded that the only course for their nation was to become militarily and materially equal to Western countries like the United States. In 1868, therefore, Japan began one of the most ambitious and enormous undertakings ever attempted by a nation: to transform itself into a modern world power in the space of only a few years. The Japanese abandoned feudalism and completely restructured the nation's political, military, and educational institutions. And they built many factories that began to manufacture modern ships, guns, and other weapons. ˉ

With these weapons, Japan began its career as an aggressor nation. The powerful new Japanese army fought wars against China (1894–1895) and Russia (1904–1905), winning both conflicts. From the Chinese, Japan gained the island of Formosa (now Taiwan), south of Japan; from the Russians, it gained control of Korea, located only a few miles west of the Japanese home islands. After defeating Russia, the Japanese bragged openly that they had destroyed the myth of the supposed superiority of the white race.

The surprised Western countries now realized that Japan was a real and quite threatening military power in the Far East. Accordingly, thereafter, whenever possible, they tried to limit that power. In 1922, shortly after the end of World War I, an international conference was held in Washington, D.C., to establish limits on weapons. One of the resolutions voted on by the Western powers placed a limit on the number of warships Japan could build. According to the agreement, for every five warships built by the United States, Britain could also build five, but Japan could build only three. Once again humiliated, the angry Japanese were now more convinced than ever that the United States and its allies wanted to keep Japan weak and submissive.

Japan seemed anything but submissive in the years that followed, however. In 1931, it invaded the Chinese province of Manchuria, and in 1936–1937, it moved into the Chinese heartland and joined the Axis, an alliance with the European fascist powers Germany and Italy. The Japanese wanted to continue their empire-building by taking over most (or all) of Southeast Asia. However, they recognized an important obstacle to their goal—the United States, which had many political and economic interests in the region, especially in the Philippines. Sooner or later, they believed, they would have to confront the Americans.

That fateful confrontation came in 1941. In July, the Japanese marched troops into Indochina (now Vietnam) to seize the area's vast stretches of rice paddies. In response, the American president, Franklin D. Roosevelt, sternly warned the Japanese to get out. When they refused, he ordered that all Japanese money invested in American banks be frozen (locked up and rendered inaccessible). This meant that the Japanese could not use their own money to buy important supplies and armaments. Other countries followed Roosevelt's lead and froze more Japanese investments. The enraged Japanese leaders now decided that there was only one way Japan could continue to survive and prosper. It had to eliminate the United States as an economic and military threat; in the name of honor, Japan must attack.

In the following months, the United States continued to express its public opposition to Japanese aggression. But the Americans still hoped to avoid war. They attempted to create a diplomatic solution, not realizing that the Japanese had already made up their minds to fight. Even while peace talks between the two countries were going on, the Japanese were secretly assembling a huge fleet. The fleet's targets were the American naval and air bases on the Hawaiian island of Oahu and the U.S. Pacific fleet stationed at Pearl Harbor, on the island's southern flank. By wiping out U.S. military forces in the Pacific, it was thought, the Japanese would cripple and humble the United States and force it to come to terms with Japan.

The mighty Japanese fleet was commanded by Admiral Chuichi Nagumo. The best estimates by historians suggest that the fleet contained 6 aircraft carriers, 2 battleships, 2 heavy cruisers, 1 light cruiser, 9 destroyers, 3 submarines, 8 tankers, and 432 planes. In addition, an advance force of 28 submarines was dispatched; their mission was to destroy any American ships that attempted to enter or leave Pearl Harbor during and immediately after the attack. On November 26, 1941, Nagumo's secret armada departed from Japan's Kuril Islands. Maintaining radio silence so as not to warn American planes and ships, the force headed eastward toward the Hawaiian Islands. On December 5, at a secret rendezvous point in the Pacific north of Hawaii, the fleet received the coded radio message "Climb Mount Niitaka." This was the order to proceed with the surprise attack.

Japanese Concerns About the Plan

The operation had obviously been extremely well thought out and well organized; if it hadn't been, such a large task force would not have been able to proceed so far under the cloak of nearly complete secrecy. Nevertheless, even after the mission was well under way, various Japanese officers involved expressed misgivings or worries about its efficiency and likelihood of success. For example, Isoroku Yamamoto, the supreme commander of Japan's fleets, did not like the idea of sending so many submarines in advance of the main fleet. He worried that they might be too easily detected and tip off the Americans to the assault. But his superiors in Tokyo, who wrongly believed that the subs would do more damage than airpower, overruled him.

Another Japanese officer, Gunichi Mikawa, commander of the battleships and cruisers in the task force, was worried that he did not have enough battleships. "Frankly, I was apprehensive," he later recalled.

> With just two battleships . . . under my command, I was operating with no margin of security at all. Our carriers were for the most part still untested, but I knew what fourteen- and sixteen-inch shells could do. I feared interception at sea [by American warships] and possible surface action . . . and I was convinced that my . . . ships would be inadequate to protect our carriers in case the U.S. fleet closed in.[2]

Fortunately for Mikawa, the scenario he feared never transpired.

Even some of the Japanese pilots felt the plan had flaws. On the morning of November 23, Nagumo ordered all officers, commanders, and pilots in the fleet to assemble on his command vessel, the aircraft carrier *Akagi*, for a discussion of the details of the attack. One speaker, Lieutenant Commander Kenjiro Ono, explained that the pilots needed to maintain radio silence whenever possible, but if they experienced engine failure or some other serious problem, they could briefly radio their positions to the fleet. At this point, the leader of the Eleventh Dive Bombing Group leapt to his feet and cried, "I object to this plan of breaking radio silence no matter what the reasons might be at the moment of such a decisive battle which is to do or die for Japan!" Turning to his pilots, he asked, "What about this? Why don't we die in silence if our engines conk out?"[3] The commander went on to suggest that the fleet should not respond to any appeals for help, even after the end of the attack. A few minutes later, the pilots agreed that they would gladly die for their country rather than risk giving away the fleet's position to the enemy. Such was the power of the feudal warrior ethic that had been instilled in countless generations of Japanese men and still remained strong despite the demise of feudalism itself in Japan.

Like Sitting Ducks

With all concerns laid to rest, early in the morning of December 7, the Japanese planes lifted off their carriers and headed for Pearl Harbor. Mitsuo Fuchida, commander and leader of the attackers, flew ahead of the other planes to scout the target. He arrived high over Oahu at 7:53 A.M. and saw the American ships lined up like sitting ducks below.

On that Sunday morning, all but three of the huge warships of the U.S. Pacific fleet lay anchored at Pearl. The USS *Arizona*, *West Virginia*, *Oklahoma*, *California*, *Maryland*, and many other heavily armored vessels, along with smaller cruisers and destroyers, crowded around the harbor's docks. Altogether, ninety-six ships were anchored at the American naval base. (Missing that morning were the *Colorado*, in dry docks on the U.S. west coast, and the aircraft carriers *Lexington* and *Enterprise*, which were at sea.) Rows of military barracks, administrative and maintenance buildings, and a hospital, as well as civilian houses, stretched along the coast to the harbor. And nearly four hundred American bombers and fighter planes were parked on nearby air bases: Hickam Field, located just south of Pearl;

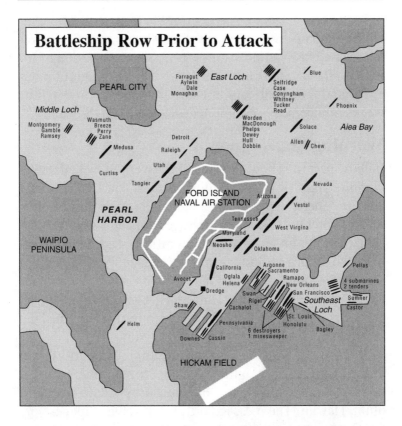

Battleship Row Prior to Attack

PEARL CITY

Middle Loch

Montgomery
Gamble
Ramsey

Wasmuth
Breeze
Perry
Zane

Medusa

Farragut
Aylwin
Dale
Monaghan

East Loch

Blue

Selfridge
Case
Conyngham
Whitney
Tucker
Read

Phoenix

Worden
MacDonough
Phelps
Dewey
Hull
Dobbin

Detroit

Solace

Allen Chew

Aiea Bay

Raleigh

Curtiss

Utah

Tangier

FORD ISLAND
NAVAL AIR STATION

Arizona

Nevada

PEARL
HARBOR

Tennessee

Vestal

West Virginia

WAIPIO
PENINSULA

Maryland

Neosho

Oklahoma

California

Avocet

Dredge

Argonne
Sacramento

Oglala
Helena

Swan

Rigel

Ramapo

New Orleans

San Francisco

Pelias

4 submarines
2 tenders

Sumner

Castor

Southeast
Loch

Shaw

Cachalot

St. Louis

Honolulu

Bagley

Helm

Pennsylvania

6 destroyers
1 minesweeper

Downes

Cassin

HICKAM FIELD

Bellows Field, in southeastern Oahu; Wheeler Field, in the center of the island; Kaneohe Naval Station, on Oahu's eastern coast; and Ewa Marine Corps Air Station, near the southwestern coast. It was clear to Fuchida that none of the ships or bases visible to him was on alert. Excitedly, he radioed back to the other Japanese planes, "Tora! Tora! Tora!" ("Tiger! Tiger! Tiger!"), which signified the successful achievement of complete surprise.

Fuchida's assessment that the Americans were unprepared for the oncoming assault was right on the mark. The enormous scope of the disaster was due in large measure to the fact that almost no one expected it. By 7:00 A.M. on December 7, some American personnel at the Pearl Harbor base were already eating breakfast or getting ready for church. But most were still asleep or lounging in their bunks. The general mood was calm because no one on the base had any reason to suspect trouble from any nation, including Japan. Everyone knew that American-Japanese relations had been strained since the Japanese invasion of Indochina the previous July. But Japan was thousands of miles away, and the Americans at Pearl assumed there would be weeks of advance notice if Hawaii were to be threatened.

Warning Signs Ignored

In retrospect, it is now clear that there were a few tantalizing warning signs of the impending assault. But U.S. officials and the American personnel assigned to spy on the Japanese and interpret their decoded messages did not take them seriously, did not understand their significance, or failed to inform the proper authorities in time. In January 1941, for example, U.S. ambassador to Japan Joseph Grew heard a rumor about a possible attack on Hawaii. He passed it along to his superiors in Washington, D.C. Apparently, they assumed the information was not reliable and ignored it.

A more ominous piece of information came to light in September 1941 when the navy department intercepted a message sent from Tokyo to the Japanese consulate in Honolulu, Hawaii. The message ordered the chief Japanese official there to report regularly on the number, kinds, and movements of U.S. ships at Pearl Harbor. The chief of the Far Eastern sector of U.S. Army intelligence, Colonel Rufus Bratton, received a copy of the message and considered it important. "The Japanese were showing unusual interest in the port of Honolulu,"[4] he said later. However, Bratton's immediate superiors felt there was nothing to the message and failed to pass it along to Husband E. Kimmel, commander of the U.S. fleet. Moreover, even if Kimmel had seen the message, in all likelihood he would not have assumed that an attack on Hawaii was imminent. After all, there had been no concrete indications that the Japanese were mounting a major naval operation.

Even more suspicious information surfaced a few days before the attack. On December 4, Peter Shepherd, a British air force technician, who was on a mission in Indochina, heard from a Japanese engineer that an attack in Hawaii was imminent; however, his report, like Grew's and Bratton's, was ignored. Then, early in the morning of December 7, the day of the attack, a Japanese message was intercepted by American intelligence personnel. It instructed Japan's ambassador in Washington, D.C., to inform the U.S. government at precisely 1:00 P.M. Eastern time that the Japanese were breaking off relations with the United States; furthermore, the ambassador was to destroy his code machine. "Again," writes historian Ronald H. Spector,

> it was Colonel Bratton who grasped the significance of the message. He was struck by the fact that it was to be delivered on a Sunday and that Tokyo had, for the first time, specified a precise hour. The colonel was convinced that the delivery time was intended to coincide with a Japanese attack on some American installation in the Far East, probably the Philippines. . . . Bratton frantically attempted to reach [Army] Chief of Staff [George C.] Marshall and his assistants but was unable to reach the general for almost an hour because Marshall had gone for his Sunday morning horseback ride.[5]

Two and a half hours later, Bratton finally showed Marshall the messages, and the chief of staff ordered that a warning be transmitted to U.S. bases in the Far East. Because of some technical foul-ups, however, the warning was not marked "Priority" and did not reach Hawaii until shortly after the attack was over.

"This Is No Drill!"

These American misjudgments and mistakes played right into the hands of Japanese war planners and ensured that the attack would be a devastating surprise. At 7:02 A.M. Hawaii time on the morning of December 7, an army air corps radar operator detected a large group of planes approaching Oahu from the north at a distance of about 137 miles. The operator quickly telephoned his duty officer, Lieutenant Kermit Tyler. Tyler knew that a flight of American B-17 bombers had left California on December 6 and were due to arrive that morning on Oahu. Thinking that these were the planes that had been sighted, he told the radar man, "Don't worry about it."[6]

Tyler and his co-workers had no way of knowing that the approaching planes were the Japanese attack craft that had followed their lead pilot, Fuchida, to Oahu. At about 8:00 A.M., this squadron, numbering 189 planes, swarmed like angry hornets over Oahu's picturesque extinct volcano, Diamond Head, and swooped down on the unsuspecting Americans. The planes struck first at Ford Island, occupying the harbor's center, which was the site of the U.S. Naval Air Station. At that moment, Seaman First Class Short was writing Christmas cards at his machine-gun station aboard the USS *Maryland*, which lay anchored near the island's eastern shore. He later recalled,

> Suddenly I noticed planes diving on the Naval Air Base nearby. At first I thought they were our planes just in mock diving practice attack, but when I saw smoke and flames rising from a building, I looked closer and saw that they were not American planes.[7]

Seconds later, many American servicemen in the harbor area heard a loudspeaker blast the urgent and now famous words of a navy operations officer, Logan Ramsey: "Air Raid Pearl Harbor! This Is No Drill!"[8]

Assault on Battleship Row

No sooner had these words been spoken when torpedo planes and dive-bombers began raining explosives on the warships clustered in the section of the harbor known as Battleship Row. As many sailors began running for their battle stations and suddenly realized the attacking planes were Japanese, many were bewildered. First reactions were typified by that of a seaman aboard the destroyer *Monaghan*. "Hell," he quipped, "I didn't even know they were sore at us!"[9] He was but one of many startled American sailors who scrambled to mount a defense but found themselves hindered by deafening noise, smoke, flames, and mass confusion. The Japanese attackers roamed at will, spreading a wave of destruction.

The assault on the ships could be seen for miles. Edwin

T. Layton, chief intelligence officer of the Pacific fleet, watched it in horror as he raced in a Cadillac roadster through Honolulu on his way to Pearl. At the same time, Admiral Kimmel, whose subordinates had earlier failed to show him the intercepted Japanese message, was in his home on a hill overlooking the harbor. Suddenly, his duty officer, Commander Vincent Murphy, rushed in and told him, "There's a message from the signal tower saying the Japanese are attacking Pearl Harbor, and this is no drill!"[10] Fumbling to button his shirt, Kimmel ran into his garden and watched helplessly as, one by one, the American warships were struck by bombs.

Some of the worst damage of all was done to the USS *Arizona*, which took a hit from a 1,760-pound bomb in its forward section. One eyewitness saw the ship "lift out of the

First-Wave Attack

Kate high-level bombers
Kate torpedo bombers
Val dive-bombers
Zero fighters
Bombing and strafing targets

OAHU

Haleiwa Field
Schofield Barracks
Wheeler Field
Kaneohe Naval Air Station
Pearl Harbor
Bellows Field
Hickam Field
Ewa Field
Honolulu
Barbers Point
Fort Kamehameha
Ford Island
Battleship Row

water, then sink back down—way down."[11] The bomb's impact was further magnified when it set off the vessel's ammunition stores, producing a monstrous fireball and a column of smoke that billowed more than three thousand feet into the air. On the bridge, Rear Admiral Isaac C. Kidd and Captain Franklin Van Valkenburgh died instantly, while below them on the second deck the members of the ship's band vanished in the explosion. Along with them, more than a thousand sailors were obliterated in one agonizing moment. The blast that doomed the *Arizona* was so enormous that it blew hundreds of sailors off their feet and into the sea. Flight leader Fuchida experienced its effects high overhead. "We were about to begin our second bombing run," he later remembered,

> when there was a colossal explosion in Battleship Row. A huge
> column of dark red smoke rose to 1,000 meters. It must have been
> the explosion of a ship's powder magazine. The shock wave was
> felt even in my plane, several miles away from the harbor."[12]

Like sharks sensing spilled blood, more Japanese fighters closed in and rained a barrage of bombs on the doomed *Arizona*. Fewer than three hundred of its crew of some fifteen hundred made it out alive.

Massive explosions repeatedly rocked other ships as well. U.S. Commander Jesse Kenworth, serving aboard the *West Virginia*, recalled,

> As I reached the upper deck, I felt a very heavy shock and heard
> a loud explosion and the ship immediately began to list to port.
> Oil and water descended on the deck and by the time I had
> reached the boat deck, the shock of two more explosions on the
> port side was felt. As I attempted to get to the Conning Tower over
> decks slippery with oil . . . I felt the shock of another heavy explosion.[13]

Another huge war vessel, the *Oklahoma*, was hit by five torpedoes and quickly capsized, turning bottom up and taking four hundred men to their deaths. In addition, the *California*, *Maryland*, *Tennessee*, and many other ships sustained heavy damage and numerous casualties. Many sailors jumped from their sinking ships in desperation, only to be burned to death in a mass of blazing oil that covered the surface of the harbor. Bill Steedly, of the USS *Vestal*, was one of the lucky ones to escape this fate. "After my shirt was burned off," he later said, "I swam out of the fire and saw a piece of timber floating by. I swam over and got my arm around it, and, with the other arm, paddled away from the burning oil."[14]

The Airfields Under Fire

Meanwhile, the relentless attackers destroyed nearly all the planes on the airfields, making it impossible for the Americans to muster a credible counterattack. At Hickam Field, the Japanese scored direct hits on the engineering building, then attacked the hangars and American planes. Ironically, to avoid ground-based sabotage, the planes had been parked wingtip to wingtip, but this made them easier to destroy from the air.

Some attackers repeatedly strafed the base's new barracks. There, Private Ira Southern ran to the window in time to see a warplane drop a bomb on the engine repair shop across the street, utterly destroying the structure. Just sec-

The Japanese attack on Hickam Field destroyed many of its planes, which were parked wingtip to wingtip in an effort to protect them from a ground attack.

onds later, another plane zeroed in on the barracks itself. A bomb smashed through a window, blasted a huge hole in the floor, and sent bits of deadly shrapnel flying in all directions. Luckily unscathed, Southern made his way to the supply room, where he and several other men collected some rifles, ran outside, and began firing at the attacking planes.

They were not the only base personnel risking everything to fight back any way they could. "Green troops under fire acted like veterans and displayed amazing courage," air force historian Leatrice R. Arakaki recalls.

> A corporal sped across the parade ground to help man a machine gun that was entirely in the open without any protection whatsoever. Halfway there, he was strafed by a low-flying Japanese plane. Mortally wounded, he kept on trying to reach that machine gun but fell dead on the way. Time and again, as the machine gunners fell, others rushed to take their places.[15]

These heroic efforts were not enough to save the base. Eighteen of Hickam's fifty-seven planes were totally destroyed and most of the others damaged. In addition, 121 base personnel were killed and 274 wounded. The other airfields also suffered. At Wheeler, fifty-three planes were lost and thirty damaged, with thirty-seven deaths; at Kaneohe, there were thirty-three lost planes and eighteen deaths; at Bellows, five planes and two deaths; and at Ewa, thirty-three planes and four deaths.

Moreover, the planes on the ground were not the only ones the Japanese attacked. In an ironic twist of fate, the flight of B-17s, which earlier that morning Lieutenant Tyler had confused with the enemy planes, arrived at the height of the attack. Regrettably, they carried no ammunition and could do nothing to help. Strafed by the enemy planes, the B-17s barely managed to land safely on the badly damaged runways or in open fields.

A Lethal Second Wave

By 8:30 A.M., the attacking planes had spent their ammunition and departed. Fearing that another assault would come,

the surviving Americans desperately raced to set up antiaircraft guns and other defenses. Their fears were confirmed
when, shortly before 9:00 A.M., a second wave of Japanese
planes, consisting of 175 bombers and fighters, appeared
and mercilessly resumed the assault. The *Pennsylvania*,
Cassin, *Downes*, *Shaw*, and several other American ships
now suffered serious damage. In addition, some of the attackers flew low and fired at people running along the
ground, killing many, including several civilians.

When the Japanese finally withdrew at about 10:00 A.M.,
Mitsuo Fuchida continued to circle overhead, photographing the results of the raid. He later admitted:

> A warm feeling came with the realization that the reward [of all
> the planning and training] . . . was unfolded before my eyes. I
> counted four battleships definitely sunk and three severely dam-

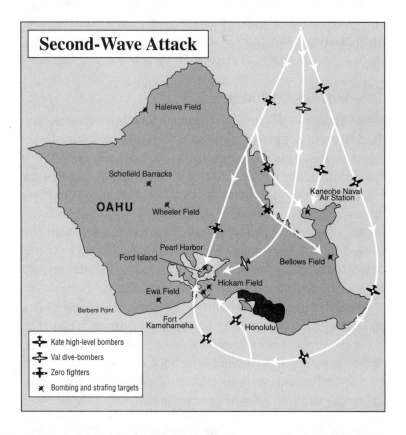

Second-Wave Attack

Haleiwa Field

Schofield Barracks

OAHU   Wheeler Field

Kaneohe Naval
Air Station

Pearl Harbor
Ford Island

Bellows Field

Ewa Field

Hickam Field

Barbers Point

Fort
Kamehameha   Honolulu

Kate high-level bombers
Val dive-bombers
Zero fighters
Bombing and strafing targets

aged, and extensive damage had also been inflicted upon other types of ships. The seaplane base at Ford Island was all in flames, as were the airfields, especially Wheeler Field.[16]

Satisfied with his and his pilots' achievement, Fuchida took pictures for nearly an hour, then turned his plane northward toward the waiting Japanese fleet.

The Japanese warplanes had left behind a scene of utter devastation. The base at Pearl Harbor lay in ruins. Giant columns of black smoke billowed from the twisted hulks of the crippled ships, and the bodies of the dead and dying sailors floated in the water and littered the docks. Fuchida's initial estimate had been conservative. Eighteen ships had been sunk or badly damaged and 308 planes destroyed or put out of action. The human toll was 2,343 Americans dead, 1,272 wounded, and almost 1,000 missing. Half of the entire U.S. Navy had been wiped out, and American military power in the Pacific was effectively paralyzed. In stunning contrast, the Japanese had lost a mere twenty-nine planes. The victory was clearly overwhelming and decisive.

Joy Versus Outrage

When the news of the Pearl Harbor attack reached Japan, the Japanese people celebrated joyously. The *Japan Times and Advertiser* ran the headline "U.S. Pacific Fleet Is Wiped Out!" The paper went on to describe the triumphant attack and claimed that Japan had "reduced the U.S. to a third-class power overnight."[17] War Minister Hideki Tojo went on the radio to announce the commencement of war with the United States. Afterward, a Japanese choir sang a patriotic song that expressed utter joy that, across the sea, enemy corpses floated in the water and littered the fields.

In stark contrast, in the United States there was only shock and outrage. One American newspaper reported, "The U.S. Navy was caught with its pants down."[18] And within hours, demands for retaliation were issued from every corner of the country. Montana senator Burton K. Wheeler exclaimed, "The only thing to do now is lick the hell out of them!"[19]

On Sunday afternoon, President Roosevelt met with his military advisers and members of his cabinet. They immediately began issuing orders for American military installations to receive heavy guard, for all amateur radio operators to be silenced, and for all private planes to be grounded. During the meeting, a call came in from Winston Churchill, prime minister of Great Britain. "Mr. President, what's all this about Japan?" Churchill queried. "It's quite true," Roosevelt responded. "They have attacked Pearl Harbor."[20]

Churchill then informed the Americans that the Japanese were at that moment attacking British bases in Malaya. In fact, the assaults on Hawaii and Malaya proved to be only the tip of the iceberg, so to speak. Reports soon poured in that Japan had also attacked the Pacific islands of Guam and Wake, as well as British bases in Hong Kong, Singapore, and many other areas in Southeast Asia.

War Declared

Roosevelt and Churchill agreed to issue simultaneous declarations of war against Japan the next day. Accordingly, at 12:30 P.M. on December 8, Roosevelt stood before a packed joint session of Congress and delivered the American call to arms. His words went out over the radio to millions of Americans and listeners in other countries. In dramatic, ringing tones, he said, in part,

> Yesterday, December 7, 1941, a date which will live in infamy, the United States was suddenly and deliberately attacked by naval and air forces of the Empire of Japan. . . . The Japanese government has deliberately sought to deceive the United States by false statements and expressions of hope for continued peace. . . . As Commander in Chief of the Army and Navy, I have directed that all measures be taken for our defense. . . . No matter how long it may take us to overcome this premeditated invasion, the American people in their righteous might, will win through to absolute victory.[21]

Ending his speech with a dramatic call for a massive war effort against Japan, Roosevelt received a thunderous ovation of clapping and cheers. Then, without a single word of substantive debate, Congress voted nearly unanimously to declare war.

Within hours, all of the country's political factions, which usually bickered among themselves, put aside their differences. In a remarkable show of national unity, Americans from all walks of life closed ranks in a show of opposition to the Japanese. Even the famous aviator Charles Lindbergh, a staunch isolationist, lent his support to the war effort, declaring,

> Now it has come, and we must meet it as united Americans regardless of our attitude in the past toward the policy our government has followed. . . . We must now turn every effort to building the greatest and most efficient Army, Navy, and Air Force in the world.[22]

As war fever spread across the United States, the country's allies, many of them also victims of the Japanese attacks of December 7, declared war on Japan. Joining the United States and Britain were Canada; Australia; New Zealand; the exiled governments of Greece, Yugoslavia, and France (countries that had been overrun by Nazi Germany); and nine Latin American countries. These nations referred to themselves as the Allies. Predictably, the other Axis countries, Germany and Italy, backed Japan and declared war on the Allies. The world was now engulfed in a state of total war.

Japan's Grave Miscalculation

With such a formidable array of nations lined up against Japan, Japanese leaders had little time to assess the implications of their attack on Pearl Harbor. They had assumed that the humiliated Americans would not have the stomach to fight and that the U.S. military threat had been eliminated once and for all. This, however, was a grave miscalculation. The Japanese had indeed dealt the United States a crippling blow at Pearl Harbor, but contrary to what the Japanese hoped and believed, the blow was not a fatal one.

Moreover, the attackers had made a number of serious mistakes and miscalculations. First, they had failed to bomb the naval repair facilities at Pearl Harbor, so all but two of the damaged ships were quickly refloated and repaired. Second, the Japanese failed to find and destroy the carriers *Lexington* and *Enterprise* and their escort ships, which were at sea at the time of the attack. These ships, along with the fighter planes they carried, had the capability of inflicting heavy damage on the Japanese.

The most important mistake made by Japanese leaders was their failure to realize the consequences of drawing the United States into the war. Japan did not realistically take into account the overwhelming industrial might of the United States. Easy access to vast amounts of oil, coal, metals, and other natural resources essential in waging war meant that the Americans would have a great advantage. The Japanese also failed to anticipate the tremendous food-producing capabilities of the United States and neglected to consider the unity and resolve of the American people during a national crisis.

Although the Japanese had underestimated the potential power of the United States, Winston Churchill had not. He had been hoping during the two long years his country had been fighting Germany that the Americans would take Britain's side in the war. Churchill knew that, once committed to the fighting, the United States would prove to be an incredibly powerful and virtually unstoppable force. Sooner or later, he declared, this force would turn the tide in the battle against the Axis nations. "No American will think it wrong of me," Churchill later wrote,

> if I proclaim that to have the United States at our side was to me the greatest joy. . . . Hitler's fate was sealed. . . . [Italy's] fate was sealed. As for the Japanese, they would be ground to powder. All the rest was merely the proper application of overwhelming force.[23]

Notes

1. H.P. Willmott, *Pearl Harbor.* London: Cassell, 2001, p. 8.
2. Quoted in Gordon W. Prange, *At Dawn We Slept: The Untold Story of Pearl Harbor.* New York: McGraw-Hill, 1981, p. 393.
3. Quoted in Prange, *At Dawn We Slept*, p. 379.

4. Quoted in Ronald H. Spector, *Eagle Against the Sun: The American War with Japan.* New York: Free Press, 1985, p. 94.

5. Spector, *Eagle Against the Sun*, p. 95.

6. Quoted in Walter Lord, *Day of Infamy.* 1957. Reprint, New York: Henry Holt, 2001, p. 48.

7. Quoted in John Costello, *The Pacific War.* New York: Rawson, Wade, 1981, p. 135.

8. Quoted in Richard Collier, *The Road to Pearl Harbor: 1941.* New York: Atheneum, 1941, p. 227. Admiral Kimmel later sent the same message to the United States, alerting the nation to the disaster.

9. Quoted in Collier, *The Road to Pearl Harbor*, p. 227.

10. Quoted in Prange, *At Dawn We Slept*, p. 507.

11. Quoted in Prange, *At Dawn We Slept*, p. 507.

12. Mitsuo Fuchida and Masatake Okumiya, *Midway: The Battle That Doomed Japan.* Annapolis: Naval Institute Press, 1955, p. 29.

13. Quoted in Costello, *The Pacific War*, p. 136.

14. Quoted in Paul J. Travers, *Eyewitness to Infamy: An Oral History of Pearl Harbor, December 7, 1941.* New York: Madison, 1991, p. 146.

15. Leatrice R. Arakaki and John R. Kuborn, *7 December 1941: The Air Force Story.* Hickam Air Force Base, HI: Pacific Air Forces Office of History, 1991, pp. 87–90. Unfortunately, there were a few exceptions to this widespread heroism. A second lieutenant lost his nerve and hid, and a few base personnel looted the PX and barracks while their comrades' attention was diverted by the attack.

16. Quoted in Costello, *The Pacific War*, p. 140.

17. Quoted in Louis L. Snyder, *The War: A Concise History, 1939–1945.* New York: Dell, 1960, p. 259.

18. Quoted in Snyder, *The War*, p. 258.

19. Quoted in Snyder, *The War*, p. 259.

20. Quoted in Costello, *The Pacific War*, p. 141.

21. Speech delivered to a joint session of Congress on Monday, December 8, 1941.

22. Quoted in Snyder, *The War*, p. 263.

23. Winston Churchill, *The Second World War.* Vol. 3. New York: Bantam Books, 1962, p. 511.

Chapter 1

Prologue to Infamy

Chapter Preface

The immediate events leading up to the epic attack on the U.S. fleet at Pearl Harbor began in January 1941 when Admiral Isoroku Yamamoto, supreme commander of Japan's war fleets, sent a letter to Japan's war minister. Yamamoto expressed the opinion that Japan could not hope to attain its goal of expansion in the Far East unless it eliminated the considerable influence of the United States in that region. And the surest and most effective way to remove that influence would be a surprise attack on the U.S. Pacific fleet.

Air ace Minoru Genda agreed with this view. Furthermore, he was convinced that airpower would be more effective than battleships in the assault on Hawaii. Genda soon found himself in charge of planning the operation and training the flight crews, endeavors that continued well into November.

Meanwhile, although the Japanese operation was top secret, American and British agents stumbled upon various clues of its existence in the last few days before the attack. British air force technician Peter Shepherd learned of the impending attack in a chance meeting with a Japanese engineer in Indochina. And an American FBI agent stationed in Honolulu, Hawaii, recorded a telephone call to Japan containing coded information from a Japanese spy living on Oahu. Unfortunately, these warnings were not taken seriously.

It is uncertain whether such warnings, even if they had been heeded, would have stopped the attack. The Japanese had made up their minds to go through with it. They were determined to humble the United States and eliminate its capacity to wage war against them. On December 6, their ambassador in Washington, D.C., gave the State Department a document that listed Japan's grievances against the United States and stated that no further negotiations would be possible; this was clearly meant to justify the coming assault.

Moreover, the strike force approaching Hawaii had a contingency plan that allowed for the execution of an attack even if surprise was not achieved.

It turned out that surprise was achieved, of course. Early on Sunday morning, December 7, Mitsuo Fuchida led the first wave of warplanes off the Japanese carriers and sped toward a date with destiny.

Advocating a Strategy of Ambush

Isoroku Yamamoto

As leader of the Japanese navy's Combined Fleet, Admiral Isoroku Yamamoto was in the forefront of the plans to attack the United States in 1941. Yamamoto held not only great military power but also the hearts and loyalty of the men who served under him. Furthermore, he had lived for an extended period in the United States and had unique knowledge of his enemy, so his opinion was highly regarded during the planning stages. This letter, written by Yamamoto to Navy Minister Koshiro Oikawa on January 7, 1941, lays out the general strategy that Yamamoto thought was the most effective way to demoralize the United States and virtually eliminate it from the Pacific sphere, namely to ambush the U.S. fleet in a surprise attack. As it turned out, this was the general strategy adopted by the Japanese government in carrying out the massive raids on Hawaii on December 7.

Although a precise outlook on the international situation is hard for anyone to make, it is needless to say that now the time has come for the Navy, especially the Combined Fleet, to devote itself seriously to war preparations, training and operational plans with a firm determination that a conflict with the U.S. and Great Britain is inevitable.

Therefore, I dare say here generally what I have had in my mind, to which your kind consideration is cordially invited. (This generally corresponds to what I verbally said to you roughly late in last November.)

Excerpted from *The Pearl Harbor Papers: Inside the Japanese Plans*, edited by Donald M. Goldstein and Katherine V. Dillon (New York: Brassey's, 1993).

1. WAR PREPARATIONS: Views on war preparations of the Combined Fleet have already been conveyed to the central authorities in Tokyo, and I believe the central authorities have been exerting the utmost efforts for their completion.

As the aforementioned request covers general major points alone, however, I think more detailed requests will be made when a real war is sure to come. Preparations are required to be made by all means will be marked as such, to which your special consideration is cordially invited. Especially, in view of the fact that satisfaction can never be attained in air strength, whether aircraft or personnel, your special encouragement is kindly requested to promote their production whenever opportunities arise.

2. TRAINING: Most of the training that has so far been planned and carried out deal with normal and fundamental circumstances, under which each unit is assigned a mission with the *"yogei sakusen"* [the strategy of ambush] as its main aim. Needless to say, the utmost efforts should be made to master it, as by so doing sufficient capabilities will be made so as to meet requirements needed in varied scenes of an engagement and a battle.

Considering a case in which this country goes to war with the U.S. and Great Britain as a practical problem, however, I think there may be no such case happening throughout the whole period of an expected war as all of the Combined Fleet closing in an enemy force, deploy, engage in a gunnery and torpedo duel, and finally charge into the enemy force in as gallant a way as possible. On the other hand, there may be cases in which various problems that have been somehow neglected in peace-time training in spite of their importance actually happen. In view of the current situation, therefore, I think earnest studies should be made of those problems.

Even when aforementioned normal and fundamental training is carried out, instead of being engrossed in overall tactical movements lacking precise consideration, unremitting studies should be made as to whether his fleet, squadron, division and ship display its fighting power to the utmost degree in every phase of maneuvers. (It will be an effective way for that end to let deviate shell firing and actual torpedo firing be included in every maneuver, and designate units at random during the maneuver to practice this training.)

If either of the British and Italian Fleets, which encountered in the Mediterranean Sea last year, had been fully trained from peace time to rouse up in the fighting spirit of "attacking enemy whenever it is sighted" and accustomed to a sudden firing, there ought not to have been a case in which none was sunk on either side in spite of the fact that the duel took place for 25 minutes. It should be regarded as a blunder that could not be allowed in our Navy.

3. OPERATIONAL POLICY: Studies on operational policy, too, have so far been based on one big "*yogei sakusen*" to be fought in a formal way. Review of numerous maneuvers held in the past, however, shows that the Japanese Navy has never won an overwhelming victory even once; they used to be suspended under such a situation that, if by letting things take their own course, there was much fear that our Navy might be dragged into gradual defeat.

It might be of some use only when collecting reference materials for determining whether we should go to war or not, but it should not be repeated by all means if and when a decision is made to go to war.

The most important thing we have to do first of all in a war with the U.S., I firmly believe, is to fiercely attack and destroy the U.S. main fleet at the outset of the war, so that the morale of the U.S. Navy and her people goes down to such an extent that it cannot be recovered.

Only then shall we be able to secure an invincible stand in key positions in East Asia, thus being able to establish and keep the East Asia Co-Prosperity Sphere.

Well then, what policy should we take to accomplish this?

4. OPERATIONAL PLAN THAT SHOULD BE ADOPTED AT THE OUTSET OF WAR:

We learned many lessons in the Russo-Japanese War. Among them, those concerning the outset of war are as follows:

a. Japan had a chance to launch a surprise attack upon the enemy main force at the outset of war.

b. The morale of our destroyer force at the outset of war was not necessarily high (there being exceptions) and their skill was insufficient. This was most regrettable, about which serious reflection should be made.

c. Both the planning and execution of the blockade operation were insufficient.

In view of these successes and failures in the Russo-Japanese War, we should do our very best at the outset of a war with the U.S., and we should have a firm determination of deciding the fate of the war on its first day.

The outline of the operational plan is as follows:

a. In case of the majority of the enemy main force being in Pearl Harbor, to attack it thoroughly with our air force, and to blockade the harbor.

b. In case they are staying outside of the harbor, too, to apply the same attack method as the above.

The strength to be used in the aforementioned operation and their assignments:

a. 1st and 2nd Carrier Divisions (2nd Carrier Division alone in an unavoidable case) to launch a forced or surprise attack with all of their air strength, risking themselves on a moonlit night or at dawn.

b. One destroyer squadron to rescue survivors of carriers sunken by an enemy counterattack.

c. One submarine squadron to attack the enemy fleeing in confusion after closing in on Pearl Harbor (or other anchorages), and, if possible, to attack them at the entrance of Pearl Harbor so that the entrance may be blocked by sunken ships.

d. Supply force to assign several tankers with the force for refueling at sea.

  In case the enemy main force comes out from Hawaii before our attack and keeps on coming at us, to encounter it with all of our decisive force and destroy it in one stroke.

It is not easy to succeed in either case, but I believe we

could be favored by God's blessing when all officers and men who take part in this operation have a firm determination of devoting themselves to their task, even sacrificing themselves.

The above is an operation with the U.S. main force as a main target, and an operation of launching a forestalling and surprise attack on enemy air forces in the Philippines and Singapore should definitely be made almost at the same time of launching attacks on Hawaii. However, if and when the U.S. main force is destroyed, I think, those untrained forces deploying in those southern districts will lose morale to such an extent that they could hardly be of much use in actual bitter fighting.

On the other hand, when we take a defensive stand toward the east and await the enemy coming on out of fear that such an operation against Hawaii is too risky, we cannot rule out the possibility that the enemy would dare to launch an attack upon our homeland to burn our capital city and other cities.

If such happens, our Navy will be subject to fierce attacks by the public, even when we succeed in the southern operation. It is evidently clear that such a development will result in lowering the morale of the nation to such an extent that it cannot be recovered. (It is not a laughing matter at all to recall how much confusion our nation was thrown into when the Russian fleet appeared in the Pacific in the Russo-Japanese War.)

I sincerely desire to be appointed C-in-C [Commander-in-Chief] of an air fleet to attack Pearl Harbor so that I may personally command that attack force.

I firmly believe that there is a more suitable man to command the normal operations of the Grand Combined Fleet after that operation, as I previously stated my view verbally to your Minister.

Sincerely hoping that you will pass a clear judgment on my request to shift me to that post, so that I may be able to devote myself exclusively to my last duty to our country.

Planning the Attack

Minoru Genda

An experienced and widely renowned pilot in the late 1930s, Minoru Genda was an early advocate of air power, especially the tactic of concentrating two or more aircraft carriers in a strike force that could deliver hundreds of warplanes on a target. At first, his ideas were ridiculed by naval officers who still cherished old-fashioned ideas about the superior capabilities of battleships and their big guns. But as Japanese leaders came to follow Yamamoto's advice about the need for a surprise attack on Hawaii, they saw the wisdom of calling on Genda to plan a carrier-based air raid. In the following excerpts from Genda's postwar recollections, he tells how he came to be involved in the planning and describes both the elements of the plan and the rigorous training instituted to prepare the pilots.

Early in February 1941, when the Flagship, the *Kaga*, was anchored in Ariake Bay (Kyushu), I received a letter from the Chief of Staff of the 11th Air Fleet, Rear Admiral Onishi, with whom I was well acquainted personally, though not under his direct command officially. In this letter he asked me to come to Kanoya at once as he wanted to see me on important business. So I proceeded to Kanoya on the following day and called on Rear Admiral Onishi at the Fleet Headquarters.

He then showed me a private letter which he had received from Vice Admiral Yamamoto, Commander in Chief of the Combined Fleet. The substance of that letter was to the following effect:

Excerpted from *The Pearl Harbor Papers: Inside the Japanese Plans*, edited by Donald M. Goldstein and Katherine V. Dillon (New York: Brassey's, 1993).

In the event of outbreak of war with the United States, there would be little prospect of our operations succeeding unless, at the very outset, we can deal a crushing blow to the main force of the American Fleet in Hawaiian waters by using the full strength of the 1st and 2nd air Squadrons against it, and thus to preclude the possibility of the American Fleet advancing to take the offensive in the Western Pacific for some time.

And it is my hope that I may be given command of this air attack force, so that I may carry out the operation myself. Please make a study of the operation.

Rear Admiral Onishi said to me, "Please make this study in utmost secrecy, with special attention to the feasibility of the operation, method of execution, and the forces to be used."

I commenced this study upon returning to my ship, and after a week or ten days, I again called on Rear Admiral Onishi and handed him my answer.

What I remember of that answer was the following:

A. Need of maintaining utmost secrecy, so as to prevent any leakage of the plan.
B. Use of sufficient force to put the main force of the American Fleet out of action for at least six months at one blow, i.e., to use all available carriers.
C. To make effect certain, the attack to be made by daylight.
D. If, owing to the extreme difficulty of torpedo attack because of shallow water, use of torpedo is found to hold little prospect of success, emphasis to be placed on dive bombing, and for that reason, the kind and number of planes aboard carriers to be changed as necessity may dictate.
E. Carriers to be selected as primary targets.
F. In short, this attack, while extremely difficult, is not impossible. . . .

Special Training Needed

The training alone must be given to the men without their knowing the purpose of the training. The men were led to train for deep and shallow torpedoing without knowing their fate, which was a little too much, but they did it. With information from the G-3 of Headquarters that both east and west sides of Pearl Harbor and Ford Island were about 40 feet deep, training was started to discharge the torpedoes so as not to go below 33 feet. I am not sure, but I think it was in the southern seas area in Kyushu that dummy torpedoes were discharged from the lowest possible altitude against the *Akagi* and *Kaga* with automatic depth calculating meters. One was good but the other was not. Since that time we had not been able to get any constant results. Some rounds were good, others were not. The rounds shot to go no deeper than 33 feet were about 40% effective.

Around June the training was still done in the old-fashioned way, using only the battleships with no help from the air force. One day I wrote a letter to staff officer Sasaki of the Combined Fleet, saying, "Stop this worthless deployed tactic training. Let the air units practice spot-attacking on land. And if the fleet training calls for air units to participate, arrange for it."

When the senior staff officer of the Combined Fleet saw the letter, I am told that he was quite angry. However, from July, I am not sure whether my letter had anything to do with it, but the air units began to train at land bases.

Finally, not only torpedo bombing was practiced but also dive bombing and low-altitude bombing training were carried out in a real way.

Around September there was a great change in the personnel and also the Fifth Carrier Division (the *Shokaku*, the *Zuikaku*, and one destroyer squadron) was assigned to the fleet.

In order to make clear the concentrated power of the air units for the Pearl Harbor attack and the operation with it, plans for special organizations and training were presented to the higher-ups for opinion, only to receive much opposition from the district and air unit commanders, but later the plans were approved. By "special organizations," I mean that all of the air units of every fleet are to be formed into two large groups with a commander in chief for both groups. Training will be carried out according to the situation of the groups. As for "special training," it is to train for the attack on Pearl Harbor as planned under the organization just mentioned. . . .

Targets and Method

In the beginning of September the chief of staff of the First Air Fleet assembled all the leaders and laid out the concrete plans. I was among the men in the group and for a week after that I was assigned to make the finished plan all by myself in the chief of staff's room without any outside help.

Furthermore, two divisions of the 3rd Battleship Division (the *Haruna* and the *Kirishima*); the 8th Cruiser Division (the *Tone* and the *Chikuma*); about eleven of the newest-type destroyer and the flagship of the 1st Destroyer Squadron were assigned as the forces to be used in the operation by

Mastering the Torpedo Runs

In this excerpt from his famous book about the Pearl Harbor attack, Day of Infamy, *Walter Lord tells about how Genda chose Mitsuo Fuchida as leader of the attack squadron and describes the crucial training for the torpedo runs necessary to inflict damage on large warships.*

Next, the training stage. One by one, men were tapped for the key jobs. Brilliant young Commander Mitsuo Fuchida was mildly surprised to be transferred suddenly to the carrier *Akagi*, having just left her the year before. He was far more amazed to be named commander of all air groups of the First Air Fleet. Commander Genda sidled up with the explanation: "Now don't be alarmed, Fuchida, but we want you to lead our air force in the event that we attack Pearl Harbor."

Lieutenant Yoshio Shiga and about a hundred other pilots got the word on October 5 from Admiral Yamamoto himself. He swore them to secrecy, told them the plan, urged them to their greatest effort.

The men practiced harder than ever—mostly the low,

the Combined Fleet. Three submarines and a few of the fastest tankers were also assigned.

The general outline of the plan after a week's study is as follows:

A. Forces to be used

  The complete forces of the 1st Carrier Division, 2nd Carrier Division, 5th Carrier Division, and the necessary forces assigned.

B. Time of attack

  At daybreak of the same day as the beginning of operations.

C. Target of attack

  1. American carrier group
  2. American battleship group
  3. Land-based aircraft
  4. All other ships

---

short torpedo runs that had to be mastered. The torpedoes themselves continued to misbehave in shallow water, diving to the bottom and sticking in the mud. Commander Fuchida wondered whether they would ever work. But Genda only grew more excited—once perfected, they would be the supreme weapon. And by early November he had succeeded. Simple wooden stabilizers were fitted on the fins, which would keep the torpedoes from hitting even the shallow 45-foot bottom of Pearl Harbor.

Meanwhile, other pilots practiced bombing techniques, for nobody except Genda was completely sold on torpedoes. Besides, the meticulous intelligence now pouring in from Consul General Nagao Kita in Honolulu showed that the battleships were often moored in pairs; torpedoes couldn't possibly reach the inboard ship. To penetrate tough armor-plated decks, ordnance men fitted fins on 15-inch and 16-inch armor-piercing shells. These converted missiles would go through anything.

Walter Lord, *Day of Infamy.* 1957. Reprint, New York: Henry Holt, 2001, pp. 14–15.

D. Method of attack
1. Torpedo and dive-bombing attack against the aircraft carriers.
2. Torpedo and water-level bombing against the battleships.
3. Strafing and low-level bombing against the land-based aircraft.

The Northern Route Best

E. Route of attack

The northern, central and southern routes were the three routes considered and there was much difficulty in determining the route to be used.

The northern route was very good as far as carrying out the plan in secret went, but there was the question of being able to supply the units at sea in the stormy waves of the northern Pacific Ocean because the operation was to begin in the winter season. This was the main reason that Vice Admiral Nagumo always insisted upon taking the southern route. However, my insistence was that from looking back into history for examples of surprise attacks, such as the Battle of the Hiyodori Pass, the Battle of Okehazama, and Napoleon's Battle of the Alps, if we do not take the northern route we will not succeed. With the aid of Rear Admiral Yamaguchi, the Commander-in-Chief understood the reason for taking the northern route. The southern route had very calm waters, the distance was only two thousand miles and it was best from the standpoint of navigation, but the chance of being spotted was too great. Therefore, ninety-nine out of a hundred agreed that a surprise attack was impossible by way of the southern route. The road to the success of the attack was opened because all efforts were restored for taking this difficult way.

In any plan which the people agree to be the most natural and best, the enemy will have the counter-attacking forces prepared. The scarcity of ships navigating in the northern Pacific Ocean in the winter was a great help to us.

There was no special characteristic nor any value in using the central route.

With the foregoing understanding, I made plans to use the northern route.

F. Assembly point before the attack

There was quite a bit of trouble in determining this port to assemble secretly a large fleet and to prepare same for an operation. The ports at the homeland and Hokkaido would not ensure secrecy. Chichi Island was too small and also easy to be spotted by submarines. It was not very close, either. We were hoping to get a port as far north as possible and during the search, we came upon Hitokappu Bay. This bay was chosen for the assembly point.

G. Supplying at sea

Out of the six carriers there were only the two from the 5th Carrier Division and the *Kaga* which were able to cruise to and from Hawaii on their own power. (I am not positive but I think that their cruising speed was 18 knots and their range 8,000 sea miles.) At any rate, because the other three ships could only cruise 60 percent of the distance, there was a need for the carriers to be supplied at sea.

In October, while the map maneuvers were carried out at Tokuyama, the *Kaga* carried out the first experimental trip. We had much confidence in the success of the attack.

Contingency and Follow-Up

H. An assault plan in case the surprise attack does not succeed

There was a necessity to consider this also, and in this case all the fighter planes will be sent out first, then the attack will be carried out after we get command of the air.

At that time we had complete confidence in the

strength of the fighter units. We thought that we could easily destroy an enemy fighter unit two or three times the size of ours in one attack. For this reason especially, we put our strength into these formation air battles.

I. The follow-up of the attack

Plans were made for the second attack, but Commander in Chief Nagumo did not approve of them from the beginning. He had the opinion that a continued attack was too much.

J. Searching for the enemy

The search for the point of origin of the American Fleet was left to central intelligence and to the submarine reconnaissance. The reconnaissance of the enemy immediate front was carried out by two Type Zero water-reconnaissance planes.

The foregoing was the basic plan of the Pearl Harbor attack. This was shown to the First Air Fleet Headquarters in September by means of map maneuvers of the Combined Fleet at the Naval Staff College.

This map maneuver was participated in by almost all of the important men in Naval Headquarters and in the various Headquarters of the Combined Fleet, but the maneuvers concerning the Hawaii attack were participated in only by the important men of the Combined Fleet Headquarters, the 1st Air Fleet Headquarters, the 2nd Carrier Division Headquarters, and the men of the 5th Carrier Division Headquarters, in a special room to ensure secrecy.

The results of the war games (the maneuver was carried out twice) were that on the first day an American reconnaissance plane discovered the attacking fleet but the attack was carried out, and that on the second day the surprise attack was successful.

Around this time I sent the staff officer for communications to the Naval Headquarters to investigate the condition of the electric wave radiation [radar] of the American aircraft in the Hawaii vicinity and to investigate the number of ships navigating in the waters of the southern Aleutian Islands and their routes in the coming winter. We found the

American reconnaissance planes from the Hawaii area were thick in the southern area and very little in the northern area. The number of planes reconnoitering the northern area beyond 2,300 sea miles from Hawaii was very few and again ships in the southern Aleutian Islands were very few. Now all the more we were determined to use the northern route for the attack. The only problems left now were the decisions concerning supplies and ability of the air units.

A Fateful Warning Ignored

Peter J. Shepherd

Stationed in Malaya, in the Far East, in 1941, British air force technician Peter J. Shepherd was ordered to take part in a covert mission in Indochina. During the mission, on December 4, just three days before the Japanese raid on Hawaii, he had a chance encounter in a restaurant with a Japanese man. In the course of a long conversation, the man revealed that he was an engineer who had earlier that year worked aboard an aircraft carrier that was bound for Pearl Harbor. The engineer also told Shepherd that the Japanese planned to attack British installations in the Far East. Shepherd made his way back to Malaya and reported what he had heard to his superiors, but the information was apparently not taken seriously. Had it been, the course of modern history might have been very different. The following extract from Shepherd's recollection, published as *Three Days to Pearl*, begins with Shepherd and the engineer finding seats on the restaurant's veranda.

H e had a grin on his face, not a malicious grin but one that denoted considerable satisfaction and pleasure. He appeared to be in his mid- or late thirties. His teeth were ridiculously even and white, and something about his complexion definitely confirmed him as some race other than Chinese. His cheeks, under prominent cheekbones, positively glowed and were tinged with a healthy pinkness. He filled the two glasses from the up-market bottle. I had no idea as to the quality of what the bottle contained, but the label stated it to be cognac. I could not drink this stuff so when my newly found friend put one of the filled glasses in my hand I inwardly groaned, then made a pretense of sipping some of the enticing amber liquid. He lifted his glass at the same time, but, instead of taking a cautious sip, he downed its entire contents in one massive gulp. Then he banged the glass on the table and treated me to yet another of his disarming grins. . . .

Communicating Through Gestures

In a moment or two the waiter reappeared with the coffee. He also brought a small dish of what I assumed to be crystallized ginger. It was sweating and almost all the sugar had metamorphosed into syrup. My friend arrived back at the table at virtually the same time. Also in the same instant it suddenly struck me that the fellow might very well be Japanese. My heart put on a special hyperactive performance for a few seconds. My problems had suddenly increased a thousandfold. . . .

I glanced at my watch. The time was 9:15 P.M. Music from the dining room drifted through to the veranda. Now it was "Sweet Sue" in a hectic quickstep tempo on violin and drums. The silver, almost-full moon kept disappearing behind clouds.

My hair was very fair, as was also my complexion. There was nothing about me that could have been seen as Gallic. Yet this thirsty gent must have jumped to the not-unreasonable conclusion that I was French. If so, it was evident that he did not speak French because from the very start he had communicated with me in sign language, gestures, and grunts. He no doubt knew that English people particularly were, perforce, something of a rarity in Indo-China, and he could hardly have expected to come face to face with an Englishman at a third-rate restaurant-cum-hotel in a fairly desolate part of Cambodia. That he almost certainly did not realize I was English did not help a lot. Even the slightest suspicion on his part could well result in words being said to, from my point of view, the wrong people. I was seized by an over-whelming desire to remove myself from his company. But there was the coffee that I had not yet finished—and the cognac, too, looked lonely in its stylish, beckoning bottle. I put on a brave face and, on impulse, topped off my coffee cup with cognac and took a generous gulp of the fortified beverage. It worked, so naturally I took another. Then I finished it off and was then ready to give my full attention to my good companion, who had begun to make certain gestures that suggested to me he was most desirous of communicating further.

The gestures and signs that he was making told me he wished to know what kind of work I did. It is easy to understand such sign language when you are receptively alert thanks to a sudden shot of brandy, and when the individual who is trying to get something across to you is determined and enthusiastic. It took me, I suppose, no more than half a minute to indicate to him that I was, broadly, in the engineering game. He held out his hands for me to inspect. They were equally as hard as mine, the fingernails trimmed right down and broken in places. He was clearly a manual worker of some kind. His further gesticulations made it apparent that he was curious to know what brand of engineering I was in, but I thought it better to withhold from him the fact that I was involved in aero engineering. To have told him that would have been to whet his curiosity even further, so I indicated that I was concerned with engines generally, along with pumps and such like equipment.

A Map of Japan

He had given the cognac a fair thrashing. It had not seemed to have affected him very much thus far, and he must have liked the taste of it. He dispensed himself another, drank his coffee in one go, then chased it down with the cognac. His face now glistened with perspiration, and his eyebrows had somehow moved up his forehead about half an inch. He had already consumed at least a third of the bottle of the cognac, and it was beginning to make inroads on his central nervous system. Yet he was still anxious to know more and, indeed, to divulge more.

With a good deal of gesturing and other appropriate body language he succeeded in imparting to me that he was a civilian engineer and employed by a big company engaged in metal fabrication for the aircraft industry. Then he again rummaged in his canvas pouch and pulled out a little book which, when opened, turned out to be a diary of sorts. He flicked the pages over, eventually finding the page he was after. It featured a map of the world that extended onto the adjacent page. He peered at it closely, then pointed to an area on the map. He looked up at me, his eyebrows still high up on his forehead. Clearly he wished to convey to me the fact that this was his homeland. Although the veranda was not overly lighted, there was enough light to enable me to see the spot at which he was pointing. It was Japan. Actually his fingers rested on the southern island of Japan.

"Ah," I said. "Japan."

He nodded his head, his face beaming with pleasure. Then he pulled a pencil from that useful pouch of his and positioned its point precisely on the southern island of Japan. There could now be no mistaking that he was Japanese. I felt numb with a kind of bleak fear.

He tapped insistently with his pencil at the map as though to make quite sure I understood his meaning. I nodded vigorously to confirm my comprehension and wished he would now calm down so that I could make my escape. But no such thing happened. Instead he turned to an empty page in the diary and began sketching something on it. Then he tore the page out and positioned it in front of me. He had, quite carefully and nearly, sketched out the islands of Japan. He pointed to himself, then to a spot on the southern island. It was there, presumably, where he either worked or lived, or both. He then did another thing with his pencil. He drew a chain of small islands extending even farther north of the main northern island of Japan. He then laughed—a kind of triumphal laugh that had in it something more like intense satisfaction rather than just happiness. Once again he pointed with the pencil at a point on one of the smallest islands he had painstakingly drawn.

He raised his head and gazed at me long and hard, his brow furrowed, perspiration trickling down his cheeks. He poured out more cognac for himself, picked up the drink, looked at it, and then put it down again. . . .

A Huge War Fleet

My Japanese acquaintance gazed at me again, as though collecting his thoughts before venturing into another session of his brand of sign language.

He spoke just one word, which sounded like "Hittocappu."

"Oh," I replied.

He banged the point of his pencil down again on the spot.

"Hittocappu," he repeated, but not so quietly this time.

"Ah-ah," I returned.

He pointed at himself, then at the spot on his drawing.

"Hittocappu," he said again, this time quite vehemently.

"Hm." I could hardly say more without blurting out some giveaway words of English.

Then he went to work on his diary and began explaining the relationship between himself and this Hittocappu place which, along with other tiny islands, was stuck out in the sea many miles north of Japan's main islands.

I sat, quiet and motionless, as he related his story by means of a remarkable miscellany of assertive grunts, hisses, and hand and eyebrow movements. He sketched in his diary such matter as he would have failed to convey to me by dint of body language alone and also used the diary to convey dates.

He had recently been engaged at the factory where he worked on the manufacture of bomb racks for aircraft of the Japanese navy. He had, along with a few others, actually been put aboard an aircraft carrier for the purpose of modifying the bomb racks on several of the aircraft carried on board. The job had been to lengthen the standard racks to accommodate new armor-piercing bombs. The work had been carried out while the carrier was sailing from Japan to

"Hittocappu," a matter of several hundred miles, as far as I could estimate from his little map. They continued working on the bomb racks and, when the work was finished on 24 November, his workmates had been taken ashore by tanker. He and one other, who apparently was next door in the dining room at this very moment, had been transferred to a destroyer and brought at speed to southern French Indo-China and then by plane to Phu Quoc, where similar bomb racks were to be modified in the same way. He and his colleague had, I gathered, arrived yesterday but had been granted overnight leave on the mainland and would in the morning be taken back to Phu Quoc to carry out their work.

At Hittocappu, he explained, it had been bitterly cold with fogs and snowstorms, but he had been able to discern the presence, in the secluded bay, of a great many naval ships, including aircraft carriers, battleships, cruisers, destroyers, and tankers. There had been talk of the carriers being loaded to capacity with planes, bombs, and torpedoes, while the presence of the tankers suggested that the whole naval armada was about to embark on an extremely long voyage. In addition to the ships, several submarines had been spotted on the surface.

The Number of Ships

As his story unfolded, my acquaintance drew in his diary little sketches of one thing and another, including planes and ships, the latter being characterized and identified by outline and relative size. He may have lost his grip on the notion of discretion, but he most certainly had not let go his hold on his engineering expertise, his neat and well-proportioned pencil sketches plainly demonstrating his above-average technical background and ability.

My interest was heavily tempered by the growing fear of being stumbled upon by either French or Japanese officials. Yet all that this fellow was divulging to me seemed to constitute such unique information that I felt compelled to follow his various meanings and explanations as best I could. To speed matters along, I topped off his coffee cup and gently pushed his glass of cognac toward him. He swallowed both drinks in quick time, then hurled the glass into the night—probably his way of denying himself any more of the potent amber poison.

Putting his now-blunt pencil down, he stared at me through those glittering slits of eyes. He was more than a little bewildered due to alcoholic intoxication, but I sensed that any second he would get his thoughts straightened out and then I would get to know more. I had no reason to dislike him; after all, I kept telling myself, he had taken pity on me. But he constituted a positive element of danger to me, and because of that I was anxious to cut adrift from him.

He grunted, "Huh," and began indicating with his worn pencil how many naval ships he had seen at Hittocappu, stabbing with his pencil on one of the pages, once for each ship. When he finally put the pencil down, I counted forty stab marks on the page. I held up my hands, fingers outstretched to indicate ten. I repeated this four times and he beamed gleefully in the recognition that I had understood his meaning. He proceeded to do a lot of nodding, but this must have made him feel dizzy, because he stopped abruptly and held his head between his hands.

I waited—very patiently under the circumstances. The band continued to play a tune unknown to me on saxophone and drums, the former blasting out in huge, rich, sonoric tones curiously interspersed with half-hearted squeaks.

Target: Purhabba

He cleared his throat mightily, once again causing others on the veranda to dart startled glances in our direction. And then he delivered the real goods, except that at the time I had little idea this was so. He picked up the pencil and drew with it an arc on the map. The arc started at the spot he had called Hittocappu, swept across the wastes of the northern Pacific Ocean, then turned to the southeast and ended in the Hawaiian Islands. He pushed the map under my nose. In the poor light I had to peer hard to see where his pencil line terminated. I knew nothing much about Hawaii, and his demonstration meant little to me at the time.

He snapped out of another short period of meditation and tapped his head—not the kind of tap that one would use to indicate that the head is aching, but rather to convey the notion of thinking. There was something in his mind that he wished me to know. Once again he riffled through his pouch and, before long, put a small magnifying lens in my hand. He pointed with his pencil at the spot where the penciled arc finished in the middle of the Pacific Ocean. I squinted through the lens but, owing to the poor light and the fact that the glass was somewhat in need of a thorough cleaning, I failed to read any of the place names that lay under it. I looked up at him, frowned, shook my head negatively, and put the lens down in front of him.

He grimaced—a facial contortion that held back nothing of his frustration and impatience. His fist came down on the table with a thump that, again, caused no little alarm among those at the other tables.

"Hawaii!" he shouted, then, again, "Hawaii!"

I nodded in agreement, having no intention of upsetting him further.

"Hawaii!" he said again, though this time in a confidentially sly and much less noisy manner. Then he tapped his head in the way he had done a few moments before—as someone does when indicating that they are of the opinion and of a particular belief. He leaned over the table toward me, raised his black eyebrows, and smiled knowingly. Perspiration stood out in miniature globules on his furrowed brow. He breathed in, then held his breath for a few seconds. Then, thrusting his head even closer to mine, he said, "Purhabba." The word came out in a low whisper.

I nodded, though I had no idea what he was talking about. He opened his eyes as wide as their natural geometry permitted. They glinted as with intense excitement and satisfaction. "Purhabba," he repeated. Then he pointed at his sketches depicting the ships he had seen at the place he had called Hittocappu; and he moved his pencil along the wide sweeping arc, starting at Hittocappu and finishing at the

place he had first called Hawaii and then Purhabba. He then
sat back, evidently pleased that he had gotten his thoughts
and notions off his chest. But he was not yet entirely
through. Seizing the pencil again, he poised it over the
Hawaiian end of the arc, then proceeded to move it repeatedly up and down over the spot. Then he suddenly spread
his arms wide and shouted, "Wugh!"

I got the idea. He was telling me it was his view that all
those ships would set out from Hittocappu, sail across the
vast expanse of the northern Pacific to Hawaii, and there attack the island he had indicated. The particular significance
of Purhabba escaped me in that I had never heard of the
place. What I did know, however, was that Hawaii was a
U.S. territory and therefore he was telling me that he sus-
pected that this Japanese armada was making ready to attack it—and evidently sooner rather than later, because he
was now pointing out imminent dates in his diary. . . .

Escape with the Evidence

The man beckoned for my attention. I leaned toward where
he was now pointing his pencil at his diary map again. Then,
with more gestures and sundry vocal explosions, he indicated to me that Japanese planes would bomb Singapore and
Malaya and that Japanese troops would attack Malaya—all
at the same time that Hawaii was, he seemed confident, being ravaged by the fleet of ships he had seen at Hittocappu.

I smiled, frowned, and shook my head as in disbelief,
though inwardly I had felt the sickening clutch of fear.

He gazed into my eyes, his lips pressed tightly together.
His eyebrows dropped and his chin assumed a fierce set. His
rather wide nostrils flared. I could tell that I had displeased
him. I filled my glass, pushed it over to him, and made a
sign for him to drink, meanwhile trying to keep a disarming
smile going. He looked at the glass, then back at me, and
then picked it up and tossed the cognac down his throat in a
courageous but unwise gesture of defiance and contempt.
Directly the liquor impinged on his internals. His face crum-
pled with acute distaste. He retched convulsively, flung him-

self out of his chair, leaned out into the darkness over the veranda rail, and proceeded to make loud, guttural, protesting noises of the vomiting kind.

This was the opportunity for me to split. I gathered together his diary, pencil, magnifying glass, and the loose pages on which he had made his little sketches. Then I ripped the double-page map from the diary, folded it with the loose pages, wrote the words "Hittocappu" and "Purhabba" and the date 24 November on one of them and stuffed these in my trouser pocket.

A Suspicious Telephone Call

Mrs. Motokazu Mori and a Tokyo Newspaper

On December 5, 1941, two days before the Pearl Harbor attack, Robert Shivers, an FBI agent in Honolulu, Hawaii, alerted a military intelligence officer, Colonel George W. Bicknell, to a suspicious incident. The FBI had been watching a local Japanese dentist and his wife, Mr. and Mrs. Motokazu Mori, for some time, suspecting them of passing along information about U.S. military installations on Oahu to the Japanese. Their phones were tapped, and that afternoon Shivers had recorded an ominous conversation between Mrs. Mori and someone at a Tokyo newspaper, *Yomiuri Shimbun.* Shivers felt that the conversation indicated something important was about to happen, and Bicknell agreed. But when Bicknell approached his superiors, they dismissed his concerns, which history has shown were very well founded. The incident is only one of several cryptic warnings about the impending attack that were summarily ignored. Following is a transcript of Mrs. Mori's telephone conversation as quoted in A.A. Hoehling's *The Week Before Pearl Harbor.*

(F rom Japan) Hello, is this Mori?
(from Honolulu) Hello, this is Mori.
I am sorry to have troubled you. Thank you very much.
Not at all.
I received your telegram and was able to grasp the essen-

Excerpted from *The Week Before Pearl Harbor*, edited by A.A. Hoehling (New York: Norton, 1963).

tial points. I would like to have your impressions on the conditions you are observing at present. Are airplanes flying daily?

Yes, lots of them fly around.

Are they large planes?

Yes, they are quite big.

Are they flying from morning till night?

Well, not to that extent, but last week they were quite active in the air.

I hear there are many sailors, there, is that right?

There aren't so many now. There were more in the beginning part of this year and the ending part of last year.

Is that so?

I do not know why this is so, but it appears that there are very few sailors here at present.

What About Local Japanese?

Are any Japanese people there holding meetings to discuss U.S.-Japanese negotiations being conducted presently?

No, not particularly. The minds of the Japanese here appear calmer than expected. They are getting along harmoniously . . . we are not hated or despised. The soldiers here and we get along very well. All races are living in harmony. . . .

Although there is no munitions industry here engaged in by the Army, civilian workers are building houses for the Army personnel. Most of the work here is directed toward building houses of various sorts. There are not enough carpenters, electricians and plumbers . . .

Are there many big factories there?

No, there are no factories but a lot of small buildings of various kinds are being constructed. . . .

What about searchlights?

Well, not much to talk about.

Do they put searchlights on when planes fly about at night?

No. . . .

Are there any Japanese people there who are planning to evacuate Hawaii?

There are almost none wishing to do that.

What is the climate there now?

These last few days have been very cold with occasional rainfall, a phenomenon very rare in Hawaii. Today the wind is blowing very strongly, a very unusual climate. . . .

Here is something interesting. Litvinov, the Russian Ambassador to the United States, arrived here yesterday. I believe he enplaned for the mainland today. He made no statements on any problems. . . .

Strange Talk of Flowers

Do you know anything about the United States fleet?

No, I don't know anything about the fleet. Since we try to avoid talking about such matters, we do not know much about the fleet. At any rate the fleet here seems small. I don't know if all of the fleet has done this, but it seems that the fleet has left here.

Is that so? What kind of flowers are in bloom in Hawaii at present?

Presently the flowers in bloom are fewest out of the whole year. However, the hibiscus and the poinsettia are in bloom now. [Shivers and Bicknell believed that this strange talk of flowers was code designed to give information about the fleet without making an eavesdropper suspicious. Why else would the newspaper pay $15 a minute, a large sum at the time, to learn horticultural facts that could be found in any gardening book?] . . .

Do you feel any inconvenience there due to the suspension of importation of Japanese goods?

Yes, we feel the inconvenience very much. There are no Japanese soy, and many other foodstuffs which come from Japan. . . . Japanese chrysanthemums are in full bloom here, and there are no herring roe for this year's New Year's celebration.

How many first-generation Japanese are there in Hawaii according to last surveys made?

About 50,000. . . .

Any first-generation Japanese in the Army?

No, they do not draft any first-generation Japanese.

Is that right, that there are 1,500 [second-generation] in the Army?

Yes, this is true up to the present, but may increase since more will be inducted in January.

Thank you very much.

Not at all. I'm sorry I couldn't be of much use.

Oh no, that was fine.

Last-Minute Messages Fail to Avert War

Franklin D. Roosevelt and the Japanese Government

On November 26, 1941, the U.S. Secretary of State gave the
Japanese government a ten-part message that outlined the
American position on the tense situation in the Far East and
urged a peaceful resolution of the two countries' differences.
No answer was forthcoming, so on December 6, only hours
before the attack on Hawaii, U.S. president Franklin D. Roosevelt sent a follow-up message to the Japanese emperor,
again calling for restraint. That same afternoon, the Japanese
ambassador in Washington, D.C., finally delivered the over-
due answer to the November 26 message; this Japanese document, often called the Fourteen-Part Message, was an arro-
gant, belligerent condemnation of U.S. policies. Thus,
although each government officially contacted the other at the
last minute, the messages were at cross-purposes, and in any
event, the Japanese had already made up their minds to
attack; so there was no chance of averting war. The two messages of December 6 follow. Special note should be taken of
the way the Japanese document lists many grievances Japan
has with the United States and its allies and concludes that no
further negotiations will help resolve matters; the message
was, therefore, little more than an attempt to justify the
impending attacks in the Far East.

Excerpted from "Message from the President of the United States to the Emperor of
Japan," December 6, 1941, and "The Fourteen Part Message from Japan to the United
States," December 6, 1941, *Department of the State Bulletin*, December 13, 1941.

President Roosevelt to the Emperor of Japan:

Almost a century ago the President of the United States addressed to the Emperor of Japan a message extending an offer of friendship of the people of the United States to the people of Japan. That offer was accepted, and in the long period of unbroken peace and friendship which has followed, our respective nations, through the virtues of their peoples and the wisdom of their rulers have prospered and have substantially helped humanity.

Only in situations of extraordinary importance to our two countries need I address to Your Majesty messages on matters of state. I feel I should now so address you because of the deep and far-reaching emergency which appears to be in formation.

Developments are occurring in the Pacific area which threaten to deprive each of our nations and all humanity of the beneficial influence of the long peace between our two countries. Those developments contain tragic possibilities.

The people of the United States, believing in peace and in the right of nations to live and let live, have eagerly watched the conversations between our two Governments during these past months. We have hoped for a termination of the present conflict between Japan and China. We have hoped that a peace of the Pacific could be consummated in such a way that nationalities of many diverse peoples could exist side by side without fear of invasion; that unbearable burdens of armaments could be lifted for them all; and that all peoples would resume commerce without discrimination against or in favor of any nation.

I am certain that it will be clear to Your Majesty, as it is to me, that in seeking these great objectives both Japan and the United States should agree to eliminate any form of military threat. This seemed essential to the attainment of the high objectives.

More than a year ago Your Majesty's Government concluded an agreement with the Vichy Government by which five or six thousand Japanese troops were permitted to enter into Northern French Indo-China for the protection of Japanese troops which were operating against China farther north. And this Spring and Summer the Vichy Government permitted further Japanese military forces to enter into Southern French Indo-China for the common defense of French Indo-China. I think I am correct in saying that no attack has been made upon Indo-China, nor that any has been contemplated.

During the past few weeks it has become clear to the world that Japanese military, naval and air forces have been sent to Southern Indo-China in such large numbers as to create a reasonable doubt on the part of other nations that this continuing concentration in Indo-China is not defensive in its character.

Because these continuing concentrations in Indo-China have reached such large proportions and because they extend now to the southeast and the southwest corners of that Peninsula, it is only reasonable that the people of the Philippines, of the hundreds of Islands of the East Indies, of Malaya and of Thailand itself are asking themselves whether these forces of Japan are preparing or intending to make attack in one or more of these many directions.

I am sure that Your Majesty will understand that the fear of all these peoples is a legitimate fear inasmuch as it involves their peace and their national existence. I am sure that Your Majesty will understand why the people of the United States in such large numbers look askance at the establishment of military, naval and air bases manned and equipped so greatly as to constitute armed forces capable of measures of offense.

It is clear that a continuance of such a situation is unthinkable.

None of the peoples whom I have spoken of above can sit either indefinitely or permanently on a keg of dynamite.

There is absolutely no thought on the part of the United States of invading Indo-China if every Japanese soldier or sailor were to be withdrawn therefrom.

I think that we can obtain the same assurance from the Governments of the East Indies, the Governments of Malaya and the Government of Thailand. I would even undertake to ask for the same assurance on the part of the Government of China. Thus a withdrawal of the Japanese forces from Indo-China would result in the assurance of peace throughout the whole of the South Pacific area.

I address myself to Your Majesty at this moment in the fervent hope that Your Majesty may, as I am doing, give thought in this definite emergency to way of dispelling the dark clouds. I am confident that both of us, for the sake of the peoples not only of our own great countries but for the sake of humanity in neighboring territories, have a sacred duty to restore traditional amity and prevent further death and destruction in the world.

The Government of Japan to the U.S. Government:

1. The government of Japan, prompted by a genuine desire to come to an amicable understanding with the Government of the United States in order that the two countries by their joint efforts may secure the peace of the Pacific Area and thereby contribute toward the realization of world peace, has continued negotiations with the utmost sincerity since April last with the Government of the United States regarding the adjustment and advancement of Japanese-American relations and the stabilization of the Pacific Area.

   The Japanese Government has the honor to state frankly its views concerning the claims the American Government has persistently maintained as well as the measure the United States and Great Britain have taken toward Japan during these eight months.

   It is the immutable policy of the Japanese Government to insure the stability of East Asia and to promote world peace and thereby to enable all nations to find each its proper place in the world.

   Ever since China Affair broke out owing to the failure on the part of China to comprehend Japan's true intentions, the Japanese Government has striven for the restoration of peace and it has consistently exerted its best efforts to prevent the extension of war-like disturbances. It was also to that end that in September last year Japan concluded the Tripartite Pact with Germany and Italy.

2. However, both the United States and Great Britain have resorted to every possible measure to assist the Chungking regime so as to obstruct the establishment of a general peace between Japan and China, interfering with Japan's constructive endeavours toward the stabilization of East Asia. Exerting pressure on the Netherlands East Indies, or menacing French Indo-China, they have attempted to frustrate Japan's aspiration to the ideal of common prosperity in cooperation with these regimes. Furthermore, when Japan in accordance with its protocol with France took measures of joint defense of French Indo-China, both American and British Governments, willfully misinterpreting it as a threat to their own possessions, and inducing the Netherlands Government to follow suit, they enforced the assets freezing order, thus severing economic relations with Japan. While manifesting thus an obviously hostile attitude, these countries have strengthened their military preparations perfecting an encirclement of Japan, and have brought about a situation which endangers the very existence of the Empire.

3. Nevertheless, to facilitate a speedy settlement, the Premier of Japan proposed, in August last, to meet the President of the United States for a discussion of important problems between the two countries covering the entire Pacific area. However, the American Government, while accepting in principle the Japanese proposal, resisted that the meeting should take place after an agreement of view had been reached on fundamental and essential questions.

Subsequently, on September 25th the Japanese

Government submitted a proposal based on the formula proposed by the American Government, taking fully into consideration past American claims and also incorporating Japanese views. Repeated discussions proved of no avail in producing readily an agreement of view. The present cabinet, therefore, submitted a revised proposal, moderating still further the Japanese claims regarding the principal points of difficulty in the negotiation and endeavoured strenuously to reach a settlement. But the American Government, adhering steadfastly to its original assertions, failed to display in the slightest degree a spirit of conciliation. The negotiation made no progress.

4. Therefore, the Japanese Government, with a view to doing its utmost for averting a crisis in Japanese-American relations, submitted on November 20th still another proposal in order to arrive at an equitable solution of the more essential and urgent questions which, simplifying its previous proposal, stipulated the following points:

1. The Government of Japan and the United States undertake not to dispatch armed forces into any of the regions, excepting French Indo-China, in the Southeastern Asia and the Southern Pacific area.

2. Both Governments shall cooperate with the view to securing the acquisition in the Netherlands East Indies of those goods and commodities of which the two countries are in need.

3. Both Governments mutually undertake to restore commercial relations to those prevailing prior to the freezing of assets. The Government of the United States shall supply Japan the required quantity of oil.

4. The Government of the United States undertakes not to resort to measures and actions prejudicial to the endeavours for the restoration of general peace between Japan and China.

5. The Japanese Government undertakes to withdraw

troops now stationed in French Indo-China upon either the restoration of peace between Japan and China or establishment of an equitable peace in the Pacific Area; and it is prepared to remove the Japanese troops in the southern part of French Indo-China to the northern part upon the conclusion of the present agreement.

5. As regards China, the Japanese Government, while expressing its readiness to accept the offer of the President of the United States to act as 'introducer' of peace between Japan and China as was previously suggested, asked for an undertaking on the part of the United States to do nothing prejudicial to the restoration of Sino-Japanese peace when the two parties have commenced direct negotiations.

The American Government not only rejected the above-mentioned new proposal, but made known its intention to continue its aid to Chiang Kai-shek; and in spite of its suggestion mentioned above, withdrew the offer of the President to act as so-called 'introducer' of peace between Japan and China, pleading that time was not yet ripe for it. Finally on November 26th, in an attitude to impose upon the Japanese Government those principles it has persistently maintained, the American Government made a proposal totally ignoring Japanese claims, which is a source of profound regret to the Japanese Government.

6. From the beginning of the present negotiation the Japanese Government has always maintained an attitude of fairness and moderation, and did its best to reach a settlement, for which it made all possible concessions often in spite of great difficulties. As for the China question which constitutes an important subject of the negotiation, the Japanese Government showed a most conciliatory attitude. As for the principle of non-discrimination in international commerce, advocated by the American Government, the Japanese Government expressed its desire to see the

said principle applied throughout the world, and declared that along with the actual practice of this principle in the world, the Japanese Government would endeavour to apply the same in the Pacific area including China, and made it clear that Japan had no intention of excluding from China economic activities of third powers pursued on an equitable basis. Furthermore, as regards the question of withdrawing troops from French Indo-China, the Japanese Government even volunteered, as mentioned above, to carry out an immediate evacuation of troops from Southern French Indo-China as a measure of easing the situation.

7. It is presumed that the spirit of conciliation exhibited to the utmost degree by the Japanese Government in all these matters is fully appreciated by the American Government.

    On the other hand, the American Government, always holding fast to theories in disregard of realities, and refusing to yield an inch on its impractical principles, cause undue delay in the negotiation. It is difficult to understand this attitude of the American Government and the Japanese Government desires to call the attention of the American Government especially to the following points:

    The American Government advocates in the name of world peace those principles favorable to it and urges upon the Japanese Government the acceptance thereof. The peace of the world may be brought about only by discovering a mutually acceptable formula through recognition of the reality of the situation and mutual appreciation of one another's position. An attitude such as ignores realities and impose (sic) one's selfish views upon others will scarcely serve the purpose of facilitating the consummation of negotiations.

8. Of the various principles put forward by the American Government as a basis of the Japanese-American Agreement, there are some which the Japanese Gov-

ernment is ready to accept in principle, but in view of the world's actual condition it seems only a utopian ideal on the part of the American Government to attempt to force their immediate adoption.

Again, the proposal to conclude a multilateral non-aggression pact between Japan, United States, Great Britain, China, the Soviet Union, the Netherlands and Thailand, which is patterned after the old concept of collective security, is far removed from the realities of East Asia.

The American proposal contained a stipulation which states—'Both Governments will agree that no agreement, which either has concluded with any third power or powers, shall be interpreted by it in such a way as to conflict with the fundamental purpose of this agreement, the establishment and preservation of peace throughout the Pacific area.' It is presumed that the above provision has been proposed with a view to restrain Japan from fulfilling its obligations under the Tripartite Pact when the United States participates in the war in Europe, and, as such, it cannot be accepted by the Japanese Government.

9. The American Government, obsessed with its own views and opinions, may be said to be scheming for the extension of the war. While it seeks, on the one hand, to secure its rear by stabilizing the Pacific Area, it is engaged, on the other hand, in aiding Great Britain and preparing to attack, in the name of self-defense, Germany and Italy, two Powers that are striving to establish a new order in Europe. Such a policy is totally at variance with the many principles upon which the American Government proposes to found the stability of the Pacific Area through peaceful means.

Whereas the American Government, under the principles it rigidly upholds, objects to settle international issues through military pressure, it is exercising in conjunction with Great Britain and other nations pressure by economic power. Recourse to such pressure as a means of dealing with international relations should be condemned as it is at times more inhumane that military pressure.

10. It is impossible not to reach the conclusion that the American Government desires to maintain and strengthen, in coalition with Great Britain and other Powers, its dominant position it has hitherto occupied not only in China but in other areas of East Asia. It is a fact of history that the countries of East Asia have for the past two hundred years or more have been compelled to observe the status quo under the Anglo-American policy of imperialistic exploitation and to sacrifice themselves to the prosperity of the two nations. The Japanese Government cannot tolerate the perpetuation of such a situation since it directly runs counter to Japan's fundamental policy to enable all nations to enjoy each its proper place in the world.

11. The stipulation proposed by the American Government relative to French Indo-China is a good exemplification of the above-mentioned American policy. Thus the six countries,—Japan, the United States, Great Britain, the Netherlands, China, and Thailand,—excepting France, should undertake among themselves to respect the territorial integrity and sovereignty of French Indo-China and equality of treatment in trade and commerce would be tantamount to placing that territory under the joint guarantee of the Governments of those six countries. Apart from the fact that such a proposal totally ignores the position of France, it is unacceptable to the Japanese Government in that such an arrangement cannot but be considered as an extension to French Indo-China of a system similar to the Nine Power Treaty structure which is the chief factor responsible for the present predicament of East Asia.

12. All the items demanded of Japan by the American Government regarding China such as wholesale evacuation of troops or unconditional application of the

principle of non-discrimination in international commerce ignored the actual conditions of China, and are calculated to destroy Japan's position as the stabilizing factor of East Asia. The attitude of the American Government in demanding Japan not to support militarily, politically or economically any regime other than the regime at Chungking, disregarding thereby the existence of the Nanking Government, shatters the very basis of the present negotiations. This demand of the American Government falling, as it does, in line with its above-mentioned refusal to cease from aiding the Chungking regime, demonstrates clearly the intention of the American Government to obstruct the restoration of normal relations between Japan and China and the return of peace to East Asia.

13. In brief, the American proposal contains certain acceptable items such as those concerning commerce, including the conclusion of a trade agreement, mutual removal of the freezing restrictions, and stabilization of yen and dollar exchange, or the abolition of extraterritorial rights in China. On the other hand, however, the proposal in question ignores Japan's sacrifices in the four years of the China Affair, menaces the Empire's existence itself and disparages its honour and prestige. Therefore, viewed in its entirety, the Japanese Government regrets it cannot accept the proposal as a basis of negotiation.

The Japanese Government, in its desire for an early conclusion of the negotiation, proposed simultaneously with the conclusion of the Japanese-American negotiation, agreements to be signed with Great Britain and other interested countries. The proposal was accepted by the American Government. However, since the American Government has made the proposal of November 26th as a result of frequent consultation with Great Britain, Australia, the Netherlands and Chungking, and presumably by catering to the wishes of the Chungking regime in the questions of China, it must be concluded that all these countries are at one with the United States in ignoring Japan's position.

14. Obviously it is the intention of the American Government to conspire with Great Britain and other countries to obstruct Japan's effort toward the establishment of peace through the creation of a new order in East Asia, and especially to preserve Anglo-American rights and interest by keeping Japan and China at war. This intention has been revealed clearly during the course of the present negotiation.

Thus, the earnest hope of the Japanese Government to adjust Japanese-American relations and to preserve and promote the peace of the Pacific through cooperation with the American Government has finally been lost.

The Japanese Government regrets to have to notify hereby the American Government that in view of the attitude of the American Government it cannot but consider that it is impossible to reach an agreement through further negotiations.

Closing In on the Target

Mitsuo Fuchida

> Mitsuo Fuchida, the commander of the air squadron that attacked Pearl Harbor, wrote the following account after the war. He first describes the Japanese naval strike force leaving Japan on November 26, 1941; then he identifies the various crucial last-minute maneuvers and decisions leading up the assault on Oahu; finally, he recollects his and the other warplanes taking off from their carriers, reaching the target, and beginning to unload their deadly cargo.

Japan's fleet strategy for the opening phase of the Pacific War was now fixed. The defensive concepts of prewar days were dead and buried. The new watchword was "Attack!"

On the political front, meanwhile, developments were rapidly pointing toward war. On 5 November, the Government and High Command jointly decided that Japan would take up arms if diplomatic negotiations failed to achieve a settlement by the end of November. On that same day Admiral Yamamoto ordered Combined Fleet to make final preparations for war, and issued an outline of the initial operations, including the attack on Pearl Harbor. On 7 November a further Combined Fleet order tentatively fixed 8 December [Japanese time, equivalent to December 7 in Hawaiian time] as the date for the start of hostilities.

By 22 November the Pearl Harbor Task Force of 31 ships, under command of Vice Admiral Nagumo, had assembled

Excerpted from *Midway: The Battle That Doomed Japan*, by Mitsuo Fuchida and Masatake Okumiya (Annapolis: Naval Institute Press, 1955). Copyright © 1955 by the United States Naval Institute. Reprinted with permission.

in utmost secrecy at Tankan Bay, in the Kurile Islands. The assemblage consisted of a Striking Force of six fleet carriers (Carrier Divisions 1, 2, and 5); a Screening Force of two fast battleships (Battleship Division 3), two heavy cruisers (Cruiser Division 8), and one light cruiser and nine destroyers (Destroyer Squadron 1); an Advance Patrol Unit of three submarines; and a fleet train of eight tankers.

The Armada Heads for Hawaii

At 0600 on 26 November this Force sortied and headed via a devious route for a prearranged stand-by point at latitude 42° N, longitude 170° W. At this point it was to receive final orders depending upon the ultimate decision taken on the question of whether or not to go to war.

On 1 December this decision was made, and it was for war. A Combined Fleet order dispatched the following day to Nagumo's eastward moving Task Force definitely set 8 December as the date for attacking Pearl Harbor.

On 3 December (4 December in Japan [the narrative now shifts to Hawaiian time]) the Task Force altered course southeastward, and at 1130 on the 6th it turned due south to close the island of Oahu, increasing speed to 24 knots.

In the very early morning of the 7th, with only a few hours to go before the target would be within plane striking distance, the Task Force received disturbing information from Tokyo. An Imperial General Headquarters intelligence report, received at 0050, indicated that no carriers were at Pearl Harbor. These were to have been the top-priority targets of our attack and we had counted on their being in port. All of the American carriers, as well as all heavy cruisers, had apparently put to sea. But the report indicated that a full count of battleships remained in the harbor.

Despite this late-hour upset, Vice Admiral Nagumo and his staff decided that there was now no other course left but to carry out the attack as planned. The U.S. battleships, though secondary to the carriers, were still considered an important target, and there was also a faint possibility that some of the American carriers might have returned to Pearl Harbor by the time our planes struck. So the Task Force sped on toward its goal, every ship now tense and ready for battle.

Zero Hour!

In the predawn darkness of 7 December, Nagumo's carriers reached a point 200 miles north of Pearl Harbor. The zero hour had arrived! The carriers swung into the wind, and at 0600 the first wave of the 353-plane Attack Force, of which I was in over-all command, took off from the flight decks and headed for the target.

The first wave was composed of 183 planes: level bombers, dive bombers, torpedo planes, and fighters. I flew in the lead plane, followed closely by 49 Type-97 level bombers under my direct command, each carrying one 800-kilogram armor-piercing bomb.

To starboard and slightly below flew Lieutenant Commander Shigeharu Murata of AKAGI and his 40 planes from the four carriers, each carrying one torpedo slung to its fuselage. Above me and to port was a formation of 51 Type-99 carrier dive bombers led by Lieutenant Commander Kakuichi Takahashi from SHOKAKU. Each of these planes carried one ordinary 250-kilogram bomb. A three-group fighter escort of 43 Zeros, commanded by Lieutenant Commander Shigeru Itaya from AKAGI, ranged overhead, on the prowl for possible enemy opposition.

The weather was far from ideal. A 20-knot northeast wind was raising heavy seas. Flying at 3,000 meters, we were above a dense cloud layer which extended down to within 1,500 meters of the water. The brilliant morning sun had just burst into sight, setting the eastern horizon aglow.

One hour and forty minutes after leaving the carriers I knew that we should be nearing our goal. Small openings in the thick cloud cover afforded occasional glimpses of the ocean, as I strained my eyes for the first sight of land. Suddenly a long white line of breaking surf appeared directly beneath my plane. It was the northern shore of Oahu.

Veering right toward the west coast of the island, we could see that the sky over Pearl Harbor was clear. Presently the harbor itself became visible across the central Oahu plain, a film of morning mist hovering over it. I peered intently through my binoculars at the ships riding peacefully at anchor. One by one I counted them. Yes, the battleships were there all right, eight of them! But our last lingering hope of finding any carriers present was now gone. Not one was to be seen.

It was 0749 when I ordered my radioman to send the command, "Attack!" He immediately began tapping out the prearranged code signal: *"TO, TO, TO"* ["Tora, Tora, Tora"].

Leading the whole group, Lieutenant Commander Murata's torpedo bombers headed downward to launch their torpedoes, while Lieutenant Commander Itaya's fighters raced forward to sweep enemy fighters from the air. Takahashi's dive-bomber group had climbed for altitude and was out of sight. My bombers, meanwhile, made a circuit toward Barbers Point to keep pace with the attack schedule. No enemy fighters were in the air, nor were there any gun flashes from the ground.

The effectiveness of our attack was now certain, and a message, "Surprise attack successful!" was accordingly sent to AKAGI at 0753. The message was received by the carrier and duly relayed to the homeland, but, as I was astounded to learn later, the message from my plane was also heard directly by NAGATO in Hiroshima Bay and by the General Staff in Tokyo.

The attack was opened with the first bomb falling on Wheeler Field, followed shortly by dive-bombing attacks upon Hickam Field and the bases at Ford Island. Fearful that smoke from these attacks might obscure his targets, Lieutenant Commander Murata cut short his group's approach toward the battleships anchored east of Ford Island and released torpedoes. A series of white waterspouts soon rose in the harbor.

Chapter 2

Attack on Battleship Row

Chapter Preface

When Commander Fuchida and his pilots reached Oahu, it was too late for the surprised Americans to mount any credible counteroffensives. Many warplanes in the first wave converged on Pearl Harbor, concentrating most of their attention on Battleship Row, where the bulk of the U.S. Pacific fleet lay anchored. The planes often flew low, so low that numerous people on the ground later said they could clearly make out the pilots' expressions. Some planes dropped bombs from above onto the helpless vessels; others engaged in torpedo runs, releasing their lethal weapons into the water to strike ships' hulls below the waterline; and still others strafed ships, buildings, vehicles, and people with their machine guns.

Eyewitness accounts of the attack have come from military personnel and civilians located all over the area. Some were on the decks of ships when the attackers appeared. Others were belowdecks, on Ford Island, on nearby beaches or hills, in the local hospital, or in or near the city of Honolulu.

Piecing these reports together gives historians and other scholars a detailed picture of the sequence and timetable of events. The destruction began at about 8:00 A.M. By 8:30, the USS *Arizona* had exploded and sunk; the USS *Oklahoma* had been torpedoed and capsized, the bottom of its hull facing upward; and the USS *Utah* had also capsized. Eventually, the first wave of planes departed and there was a lull lasting about twenty minutes.

Shortly before 9:00, the second wave of Japanese warplanes swooped down and rained bombs on the *Pennsylvania*, *Cassin*, *Downes*, and *Raleigh*. An explosion cut the USS *Shaw* in two. And many other vessels sustained damage. By the time the second attack ended at about 10:00, Pearl Harbor was littered with wrecked ships, many of them burning and sending up thick plumes of smoke.

The Whistle of Falling Bombs

Edwin T. Layton

Edwin T. Layton, who served as the chief intelligence officer
of the U.S. Pacific fleet during World War II, was one of the
few individuals who was present both at Pearl Harbor on
December 7, 1941, and at the Japanese surrender ceremony
aboard the USS *Missouri* on September 2, 1945. At the time
of the raid on Oahu, he was stationed on that island and living
in a house on the eastern slope of Diamond Head. In the following riveting narrative, Layton provides an excellent general overview of the major incidents of the raid on the harbor
from the American point of view. He includes not only his
own memories of what he saw, but also short descriptions of
other eyewitnesses in the general area, including that of his
superior, Admiral Kimmel.

The torpedo bombers with their menacing instruments of
destruction crowned by strange wooden boxes came
looping in around Ford Island. Peeling off in pairs, they
headed toward the line of battlewagons. The raid erupted
with such sudden fury that it was vital minutes before those
on board the helpless warships grasped what was happening.

Along Battleship Row the forenoon watch had just been
piped to breakfast. Smartly drilled color parties were lined
up on the fantails awaiting the bugler to signal the hour to
break out ensigns. But the calls and the gentler sound of
chiming chapel bells drifting across the harbor were

abruptly drowned by the rattle of machine gun fire, the whistle of falling bombs, and the sickening crump of torpedo explosions.

Deadly Torpedo Runs

The first "Kate" torpedo plane raced in so low over *Nevada* that it shredded the half-hoisted ensign [flag] with cannon fire. The sternmost battleship's astonished band continued to thump out a few more bars of "The Star-Spangled Banner" without missing a beat. Like a bloated steel lance the plane's torpedo splashed into the harbor abaft of *Arizona*, which was moored ahead. On board *Maryland* a seaman in the superstructure managed to break out a machine gun belt to open fire on two approaching torpedo planes.

The round of explosions that rocked Ford Island also roused the commander of the 2nd Patrol Wing. He broadcast an alarm from the control tower at 0758: "Air raid Pearl Harbor. This is no drill." Within a couple of minutes the shrill cry of alarm was taken up by the naval radio station, which began flashing it out to the United States.

The Kates attacked in tandem, and moments later torpedoes had slammed into *Oklahoma* and *West Virginia.* High aloft, Fuchida was encouraged by "tiny white flashes of smoke [and] wave rings in the water" as the assault concentrated on the outermost of the three pairs of battleships.

[Admiral] Kimmel was still in his dressing gown at just before 0800 when he took a call from the duty officer reporting that *Ward* had stopped a suspicious sampan. Murphy was still speaking when Kimmel's yeoman rushed in to tell him that the signal tower was broadcasting that the attack was no drill.

Kimmel had not yet finished buttoning his white jacket as he rushed outside. He stood transfixed for a few moments on the neighbors' lawn where he had a clear view of the planes circling over the harbor like angry hornets. "I knew right away that something terrible was going on," Kimmel would recall, "that this was not a casual raid by just a few stray planes."

The first explosions rocked the underground headquarters of Station Hypo where Lieutenant Wesley "Ham" Wright was the duty officer that Sunday morning. The man he sent upstairs to check what was going on was Lieutenant John A. Williams, the only traffic analyst who had argued that the long radio silence of the Japanese carriers meant they were at sea. Williams must also have been the only man at Pearl Harbor that morning who was not surprised to see that the wheeling and diving planes had orange roundels on their wings. "They're Japanese aircraft and they're attacking Pearl Harbor," he came down to tell Wright in a flat voice.

Waterspouts and Black Mushrooms

My astonishment was complete when, at about the same time, my yeoman called me with the shocking news. At first I found it difficult to grasp, because the sight and sound of the fury erupting at Pearl Harbor was shut off from my house by the drop curtain of Diamond Head.

Minutes later my neighbor Lieutenant Paul Crosley picked me up in his Cadillac roadster. As we hurtled down into Honolulu, the nightmare grew larger the closer we came to the naval base, which radiated terrible explosions. I remember feeling that this was just a bad dream that could not be true.

Tall columns of smoke were rising from Battleship Row. Prompt flooding of the magazines had saved *West Virginia.* But in the first quarter hour a combined strike by bombs and torpedoes had caught the great battleship astern of her. *Arizona* erupted in a volcanic sheet of flame as her forward magazines ignited.

At the head of the row torpedoes had ripped open *Oklahoma*'s port side. She turned turtle within minutes, entombing more than four hundred crew members.

Waterspouts from bombs and torpedoes continued to burst skyward. Overhead the increasing number of black mushrooms of exploding anti-aircraft shells were a hopeful indication that our gunners had recovered from their initial shock and were fighting back. Fuchida's plane was hit "as if struck by a huge club." A few holes and a severed control

Clouds of smoke engulf the West Virginia *as sailors attempt to extinguish the fires aboard the battleship.*

cable, however, did not stop the leader's bombing run over *Maryland*. Four missiles plummeted down to become "poppy seeds and finally disappeared just as two white flashes of smoke appeared on and near the ship."

Maryland was saved by her stoutly armored deck. Like *Tennessee* astern, her inboard position also protected her. While far from unscathed, the pair were the least damaged of all the battleships. Not so the battle force flagship. At her isolated forward berth *California* took two torpedoes and was settling by the head. *Nevada*, at the rear of Battleship Row, was struggling to get under way. She had cast off her moorings and every gun that could be trained aloft was firing at the dive bombers that swarmed down on her.

A little under half an hour after the attack began, its fury began to abate when the first wave of planes flew off. Across the harbor, destroyer *Helm* ran down and damaged another midget submarine, which would later beach and a single member of her two-man crew survive to surrender.

During the twenty-minute lull Admiral Kimmel reached his headquarters at the submarine base, while Crosley and I were still fighting our way through traffic with the help of a friendly motorcycle policeman. . . .

The Second Wave of Attackers

While Admiral Bloch was telephoning an eyewitness account of the raid to the secretary of the navy, the second wave of the Japanese attack came winging in over Honolulu.

"He could look through a window," as Knox was to relate, "and see smoke and flames from the ships still burning in the harbor."

The renewal of the raid's intensity coincided with the arrival of the first of the B-17s flying in from the west coast. Unarmed and down to their last gallons of fuel after the fourteen-hour flight, the pilots nonetheless managed to land their bombers by scattering to airfields all over the island.

A hot reception also greeted the eighteen Dauntless dive bombers that had flown off *Enterprise* an hour earlier. One was shot down by our own gunfire, and four by Japanese Zeros.

Not a single navy pilot managed to get aloft as 140 Japanese dive bombers and high-level bombers swept in from the east. Battling fearful odds, a handful of army pursuit planes did climb off from Bellows Field to knock eleven enemy planes out of a sky that was now being punctuated by the puffs of antiaircraft fire.

Retaliation came too late to save the battleships. Kimmel stood by the window of his office at the submarine base, his jaw set in stony anguish. As he watched the disaster across the harbor unfold with terrible fury, a spent .50-caliber machine gun bullet crashed through the glass. It brushed the admiral before it clanged to the floor. It cut his white jacket and raised a welt on his chest.

"It would have been merciful had it killed me," Kimmel murmured to his communications officer, Commander Maurice "Germany" Curts.

Later that day the admiral would show me the bullet and explain that although the practice was to turn over all captured enemy matériel to fleet intelligence, he would like to keep it.

Nevada's Dash for Safety

The second wave of the attack was reaching its peak when destroyer *Monoghan* managed to ram a single midget submarine that was coolly firing a torpedo at the tender *Curtiss*, which was moored in the middle loch. The Japanese dive bombers concentrated their efforts on *Nevada* as she crawled past the blazing wreckage of Battleship Row. Her defiance was gamely cheered on by the men waiting to be rescued from the overturned *Oklahoma*.

Some *Arizona* survivors were picked up and helped man *Nevada*'s guns as the defiant battlewagon continued to fight off her attackers. The tugs that hurried out to prevent the listing battleship from sinking and blocking the main channel somehow managed to beach it at Waipo Point. It was the tugs' fire pumps that fought the flames that were threatening to engulf the battleship after her own fire main was knocked out by a bomb.

Nevada's dash for safety drew the Japanese bombers away from *Pennsylvania*, which was helplessly chocked up in the Number 1 Dry Dock. One bomb did penetrate the flagship's boat deck. Another bomb blew the bows off destroyer *Shaw* which was sharing the dock with the battleship and destroyer *Cassin*. The dry dock was flooded to douse the flames, but the intense heat of the burning fuel oil ignited the magazines and torpedo stores of both thin-hulled destroyers.

Ten minutes before this terrific explosion rocked the southern end of the harbor, which occurred just after 0900, Crosley and I roared up to Pacific Fleet headquarters across the loch from the dry dock. Under such terrible circumstances, with antiaircraft gunfire blasting up from the submarines, there was no satisfaction in being greeted as the "man we should have been listening to." I felt numb, and very sick.

The atmosphere was one of general shock and electric wonder about what was going to happen next. Everyone was stunned. Even my yeoman, who was normally as steady as a rock, was jittery as he handed me the intelligence log that he had been keeping. It detailed the progress of the attack and listed the ships hit so far, those that were sinking, and others that were asking for assistance. It made me feel physically ill just to read it.

Looking out of my window, it was even more horrible to see *Oklahoma* upside down and *Arizona* ablaze. Seaplanes were burning like torches on the ramp at Ford Island.

No Satisfaction Whatsoever

I knew that men were out there dying. Oil was burning on the water and the sky was a pall of black smoke. Such a terrible scene of destruction was impossible ever to forget. There was another pyre rising over the hill from the marine corps field at Ewa. My log said that Wheeler Field had been knocked out and most of its planes destroyed. Kaneohe naval air station on the west side of the island was out of commission and under attack.

Captain McMorris arrived at 0900 and immediately asked to see me. When I entered his office down the corridor I found the chief of war plans with Murphy and other members of his staff. They all looked at me as though it was a court-martial.

"Well, Layton, if it's any satisfaction to you, we were wrong and you were right," McMorris declared.

Of course I had been saying for weeks that Japan was planning aggressive moves, but it had not been my prediction at any time that they would open hostilities with an attack on Pearl Harbor. "Sir," I said, "it is no satisfaction to me whatsoever."

Inside the Danger Zone

Joseph Ryan

Navy radioman Joseph Ryan witnessed the destruction of most of the big ships in Battleship Row from various vantages inside the danger zone. After being blown off his feet while serving on the USS *Argonne*, he spent most of the remainder of the attack aboard smaller vessels endeavoring to rescue sailors who had to abandon the larger warships.

I joined the Navy in New York City on November 19, 1940. I went to Boot Camp in Newport, Rhode Island, where I got pneumonia. I had made the Class A school to be a radioman, but my training was delayed for a month due to the pneumonia. After I recuperated, I went to San Diego for 16 weeks of radio school. I completed training in August 1941, a month after the rest of my class, who had already graduated. In September, I went to Pearl on the USS *Argonne*. Now, here's the gimmick. Practically every one of the guys who went to school with me was killed at Pearl Harbor because they were assigned to the *Arizona* or the *Oklahoma*. I was spared because of that case of pneumonia.

I was stationed in Pearl as what was called a radio striker, and was transferred to the USS *Antares*, a flagship for oil tankers. In October 1941, the *Antares* was sent to Palmyra Island, where they were building an airfield. There was no fresh water on Palmyra, so they had to send water down there on a barge. They sent the *Antares* down there to tow

Excerpted from "Joseph Jerome Ryan, Pearl Harbor Survivor," www.historychannel.com, n.d. Copyright © by the History Channel. Reprinted with permission.

the empty barge back to Pearl. They didn't need a whole bunch of us radio strikers for that, so they left us on Pearl.

A brand new captain's gig came into Pearl while the *Antares* was gone. A captain's gig is a small vessel that brings the Captain ashore before his ship is tied up. There was a kid by the name of Brady and myself—we were radio strikers— and a kid who was a coxswain. The three of us got assigned to get this gig ready. We scraped and painted that thing for three or four weeks! We finally finished on December 6th and came back to Ford Island—right where all the battleships tie up—where the Lieutenant had to inspect this gig. . . .

Memories Like Snapshots

The morning of December 7th, Brady, the coxswain, and I were supposed to stand by to meet the *Antares* coming in to Pearl. At 7:30 A.M., the three of us were waiting on the quarterdeck of the *Argonne* for the call to go out on the captain's gig and meet the *Antares*. 7:30 came and went. I'm standing there, eating an apple on the deck of the *Argonne* when suddenly, dive-bombers hit out of the blue! You knew they were Japanese because they had those big red symbols on the front—we called them meatballs.

We stood there with our mouths open, watching the hangars blowing up! Formations of Japanese torpedo bombers were flying overhead with their fish—a fish is a torpedo—hanging beneath them. They let their fish go into the *Oklahoma*—I remember her getting hit. Immediately, she started to tip starboard, and as she rolled upside down, you could see guys running to keep up on the keel.

I remember the attack like snapshots. I was told to go down below-decks of the *Argonne* to get gas masks. The gas masks were in what looked like a 50-gallon oil drum, and I had to open that thing up to get them out. I got the masks, but cut my hand doing it. The next thing I remember was carrying cases of 50-caliber ammunition to the topside. I was carrying that ammunition up the ladder when the USS *Shaw* blew up. The concussion blew me right off the ladder.

I remember the Marines showing me how to make belts

of 50-caliber ammunition—that's what I was doing during one wave of the attack. You could hear the shrapnel hitting the deck around you. I also remember a Japanese torpedo plane flew over to us, let his fish go and hit the *Oglala*, a minesweeper flagship, and the USS *Helena*, a light cruiser.

Finally, there was a lull. We were called away to get the captain's gig and go to the aid of the *Nevada*, which had been torpedoed as it got underway. The *Nevada* was the only ship that got underway that day, and when it did we cheered like something out of a movie. It was torpedoed probably half a mile from where we were—she was sinking right in the entrance to the channel. We helped take wounded men off the ship in our gig. I remember one guy had a Honolulu gal tattooed on his arm, and he was all burned. His skin was loose and wiggling in the wind. It looked like she was dancing. That was sort of an eerie thing to see. There were so many burns—it was terrible. I remember picking up a guy who was swimming in the water. The whole place was burning like hell, and he said, "Take it easy, man, you're hurting my legs." We looked and his legs were nothing but a mass of blisters and burns. We took these guys off and we headed back to the *Argonne* when the second wave hit.

Expecting an Invasion

The rest of the morning we spent picking poor guys out of the oil. You know, all these battleships had been fueled on Saturday. A lot of guys were in the water after the *Arizona* blew up. The wind was blowing about 25 knots, and it set that whole place afire—that's what killed so many people.

We came back to the *Argonne* as the sun was going down. We were tied up on our captain's gig on the outboard side of this 10-10 dock. All of a sudden, everybody started shooting. Our own planes had come in from one of the carriers. There were machine gunners in the masts of all the sunken battleships, and they opened up on these planes—too bad they were our own. Those gunners strafed all 10-10 dock. I nearly got it that night! The tracers went right through the top of our captain's gig. I don't know how many guys were killed on the dock, but I know one sad thing. We went back on the *Argonne* that night to get coffee and there was a sailor dead at a mess table. I was told that a 50-caliber went through the side of the *Argonne*, hit this kid in the head and killed him. He had been trapped all day in the sunken *Utah*. I often wondered if his folks knew that he lived through the actual attack.

That night they issued us 30-caliber rifles and ammunition. They said, "You guys stay right here on 10-10 dock, and when the Japanese come in get as many of them as you can before they get you." We thought we were going to be invaded.

Being a radio striker, I was assigned to run messages by hand. You couldn't go five feet because somebody would start shooting. You wore your whites so that you could be seen in the dark, and whistled the "Star-Spangled Banner" so you'd be known as an American. Boy, it was risky; I could easily have been shot.

The View from the
Arizona's Crow's Nest

Vernon Olsen

Seaman First Class Vernon Olsen was assigned to the 50-caliber machine gun in the crow's nest of one of the USS *Arizona*'s masts. From his vantage high above the deck he had an unusually good view of the bombing runs made by the Japanese planes. Later, after abandoning ship, Olsen went to Ford Island, where again he had a panoramic view of the remainder of the assault. His brief but action-packed account comes from an anthology titled *The USS Arizona*.

I was just getting ready to go to quarters and the attack started. We looked outside and saw the planes going by. Then they rang the general alarm. I went up to the crow's nest on the after mast. They were strafing and bombing, but it don't take you long.

You crawled up the ladders as fast as you could. I was scared. Everybody was scared. Anybody said they weren't scared were crazy.

Everyone's trained to function automatically—that's what all the battle practice was for. You were almost brainwashed, but it works and you react automatically to the situation.

The ammunition was stored below the platform, but the guy with the key never got there. When we went out for battle practice, they'd pour water in them, just enough to fire so many rounds of ammunition. If you didn't have water in them, the barrels would swell up and burst. If they're not

Excerpted from *The USS Arizona: The Ship, the Men, the Pearl Harbor Attack, and the Symbol That Aroused America*, by Joy Waldron Jasper, James P. Delgado, and Jim Adams (New York: St. Martin's Press, 2001). Copyright © 2001 by Joy Waldron Jasper, James P. Delgado, and Jim Adams. Reprinted by permission of the publisher.

water-cooled they explode from being too hot. We still couldn't have fired them, because the fellow that had the keys to the ammunition [ready locker] never made it up there anyway. [With no hoses and no ammunition, Olsen and his comrades were unable to fire back at the enemy planes.]

We just stood there and watched them fly right between the masts and bomb us. You could see their faces. You could see them grinning when they were firing at us. They flew right between the two masts. Our machine gun nest must have been two hundred, three hundred feet high, so we had a bird's-eye view of it. We could see them bombing Ford Island. We felt pretty vulnerable. [The order was given to abandon the *Arizona*.]

You weren't allowed to leave your battle station before they give the word to abandon ship—that would really be

The Attackers' View

Though Olsen was located high above the ships' decks, the vantage of the Japanese pilots was even higher. In this excerpt from his riveting account of the raid, lead pilot Mitsuo Fuchida describes his view of the explosion that doomed Olsen's vessel and other deadly bombing runs.

While my group circled for another attempt, others made their runs, some trying as many as three before succeeding. We were about to begin our second bombing run when there was a colossal explosion in battleship row. A huge column of dark red smoke rose to 1,000 meters. It must have been the explosion of a ship's powder magazine. The shock wave was felt even in my plane, several miles away from the harbor.

We began our run and met with fierce antiaircraft concentrations. This time the lead bomber was successful, and the other planes of the group followed suit promptly upon seeing the leader's bombs fall. I immediately lay flat on the cockpit floor and slid open a peephole cover in order to observe the fall of the bombs. I watched four bombs plummet something. They had the speakers, and we heard it and came down. I guess I was up there fifteen or twenty minutes.

I got off there before the magazines exploded, before the *Arizona* blew, and I got a ride in the admiral's barge over to Ford Island. They strafed us all the way going over, from where the ship was tied up all the way to Ford Island. The Japs strafed the motor launches.

[Olsen could see oil burning in the water at every turn.] The oil was pretty bad. I got burned coming down off the mast. The explosions and the heat were so intense, and coming back down to abandon ship I got burned on my arms. Everything was rocking.

They were bombing the air station and everything was blowing up. It was absolute turmoil.

You could see the *Arizona* and all the battleships under fire.

---

toward the earth. The target—two battleships moored side by side—lay ahead. The bombs became smaller and smaller and finally disappeared. I held my breath until two tiny puffs of smoke flashed suddenly on the ship to the left, and I shouted, "Two hits!"

When an armor-piercing bomb with a time fuse hits the target, the result is almost unnoticeable from a great altitude. On the other hand, those which miss are quite obvious because they leave concentric waves to ripple out from the point of contact, and I saw two of these below. I presumed that it was battleship MARYLAND we had hit.

As the bombers completed their runs they headed north to return to the carriers. Pearl Harbor and the air bases had been pretty well wrecked by the fierce strafings and bombings. The imposing naval array of an hour before was gone. Antiaircraft fire had become greatly intensified, but in my continued observations I saw no enemy fighter planes. Our command of the air was unchallenged.

Mitsuo Fuchida and Masatake Okumiya, *Midway: The Battle That Doomed Japan.* Annapolis: Naval Institute Press, 1955, pp. 29–30.

They had them all in a row, two by two, tied to the quays. The *West Virginia* was tied up ahead, and the *Arizona* and the *Nevada* were close behind. The *Nevada* was under way and they beached it, afraid they'd get stuck in the channel. The Japanese had miniature subs going in and out of there.

The *Utah* capsized, keeled right over. The *Nevada* they ran aground. There was a hospital ship, the *Solace*, under way. You could see the planes fly in and drop torpedoes. They'd head right in for the ship. Mostly they were torpedo bombers. They'd drop the torpedoes that went down underwater and as they came in they blew up under the waterline. People were hurt and screaming and crying. The noise was terrible.

Abandoning the *Arizona*

Carl Carson

One sailor on the ill-fated *Arizona*, Carl Carson, was lucky to escape alive, for he had earlier been working in the area where the fatal bomb hit. As it was, even though he was standing on the ship's deck hundreds of feet farther forward, the concussion of the great blast ruptured both his lungs. Carson's graphic, chilling narrative of his experience, recorded shortly before his death in January 2001, follows.

Well, I was out on deck doing the morning chores, which you did every morning . . . all of a sudden, this plane come along, and [I] didn't pay much attention to it; because planes were landing at Ford Island all the time. And all of a sudden, the chips started flying all around me and the plane—it was strafing me . . . They went between the ship and Ford Island, and I could look up and I could see the meatball [red circle, the rising sun symbol of Japan] on the wings and I could see the pilot sitting up there . . . I ran forward and tried to get under cover. And the officer of the deck, which was one of my division officers, ordered me back out to close the hatches on the thing . . . and then another came around about the same direction and strafed us. But I don't think anybody that was out there working at the time got hit. . . .

The Ship Was a Total Loss

I went forward and went inside the ship, and then started back to my battle station and a bomb went off. I learned later it was back about turret number 4—about where I'd been working about 10, 15 minutes before. And evidently it knocked me out, ruptured both my lungs . . . And all the lights went out . . . I don't know how long I laid there. But when I woke up, I picked up a flashlight . . . and started down, into my battle station . . . They wouldn't let me in the door—the water tight door which you're not supposed to open in battle conditions—but I managed. It seemed like it was about 20 minutes . . . and I finally outlasted the guy on the other side.

And when I got into the turret, it was totally dark in there except the flashlight. And one of my division officers . . . said, "boy you're a good boy Carson." And he said that's exactly what we needed. And it was, it was no panic down there or anything. But there was smoke and water knee deep . . . and the senior division officer . . . told us to all come out on deck & help . . . fighting fire & so forth . . . but there was

The USS Arizona *explodes after being hit by Japanese torpedoes. Over eleven hundred of its crew were killed in the attack.*

nothing we could do. The ship was a total loss and the commander . . . said well we just as well abandon ship. But before I did, I run into a friend of mine . . . he was crying and, and asking me for help. And I looked at him in horror. And the skin on his face & his arms and everything was just hanging like, like a mask or something. And I took hold of his arm. Skin all came off in my hand. And there, there was just nothing in this world I could do for that boy. And that has bothered [me] all my life . . . But he died. He did die later.

"War Sure Is Hell"

Well, they gave the word "abandon ship" and we just practically stepped off on the quarter deck into the water . . . I didn't know how bad I was hurt. And I got out there about 10 feet and I guess I must have passed out. [I] went down in the water and everything was just as peaceful and nice, it would have been so easy to just let go. And I saw this bright light and something made me come to. And so I got back up to the surface of the water and . . . the oil was a fire all around . . . the fire was approaching me, wasn't but two feet from me and he reached down and pulled me up out of the water. And that man saved my life. And a motor launch came along and I either jumped or fell into the motor launch. . . . And they took me over to Ford Island. [I] walked down to the barracks with the rest of the crew . . . I guess I must have passed out because my . . . friends and shipmates took me over to the sick bay at Ford Island . . . later there was a dead shell hit right in the center of the sick bay, and it kind of brought me to and I looked over. Another shipmate [was] laying across from me in I guess the bulk head and he was holding his intestines in with his hands. And he looked up at me, and he said . . . "war sure is hell isn't it, shipmate." And I said, "yah it is." And I wasn't bleeding anywhere so I got up and walked out of there.

Chaos Below Decks

John H. McGoran

> Many of the beleaguered seamen in Battleship Row struggled
> below decks as their ships were pounded and began to sink.
> Nineteen-year-old John H. McGoran was in an enclosure
> beneath one of the big guns on the USS *California* when the
> attack began. His narrative of his experiences in the hours
> that followed reveals a vivid picture of the size and complex-
> ity of such warships and the courage of their crews when
> under fire.

The morning of December 7, 1941, was typical of any
Sunday morning aboard the battleship USS *California*.
My billet for meals was the Marines' casemate #8 (an armored enclosure for a gun) located portside midship, just
where the forecastle breaks and a ladder leads down to the
quarter-deck. Breakfast over, I took my dirty dishes to the
scullery below. Lamentably, that's the way peace ended. Just
then a sailor ran by crazily singing, "The Japs are coming—
hurrah, hurrah!" I don't remember the alarm that sounded
General Quarters. I only know that suddenly I joined in a
rush to battle stations, in No 3 turret's lower powder handling room.

Struck by a Torpedo

When hurrying to our battle stations, to reach the decks below, we were trained to jump down the hatch—instead of
using its ladder—(ladder is ship talk and most often refers
to a steep iron stairway). Then, grab onto a bar attached to

the overhead (ceiling) of the deck below and swing one's body into a run in the lower passageway. That's roughly the way I arrived at my battle station in the "lower powder handling room" where a First-class petty officer, named Allen, was in charge.

Allen was one of those old-time petty officers referred to as "The backbone of the Fleet." Now, he was busily giving orders we couldn't carry out because no one had the keys to the powder magazines (room).

Suddenly, a violent lurching shook us all, tossing us around like so many unmuscled puppets as the ship seemed to rise up a foot, then settle back. Allen grabbed at his ear phones. "We're hit," he cried. "A torpedo!"

"So what!" I thought foolishly. "Enjoy it!" The armor plating around the USS *California* was at least a foot thick.

My idiot elation was brief. A torpedo had hit us. (Three in all hit below the armor plating and made huge holes.) The fuel tank next to our port magazine ignited in flames and there we were, surrounded on three sides by powder-filled magazines.

Immediately orders came to check the temperature of the bulkhead (wall) separating the magazine from the fuel tank. We forced the lock on the magazine door and opened it. With that accomplished we discovered the covers had shaken off some of the cans containing the 14-inch powder bags and the aisle was strewn with ripped open bags of gunpowder.

A Life to Be Saved

Anxiously, I entered, walking carefully over the debris to feel the bulkhead. I returned and reported to Allen that the bulkhead was cool. Allen in turn passed the reassuring word over the mouthpiece of his headset to the bridge.

Whatever reply came back over the phones was reflected in the strain on Allen's face. He couldn't seem to comprehend, perhaps he didn't want to believe. He turned to us and almost in a whisper said, "The *Oklahoma*! It has capsized!" Frighteningly, our ship was beginning to list dangerously.

Allen received a report that our anti-aircraft ammunition

supply line had broken down from an explosion. The break was reported to be in "CL" compartment, my sleeping quarters, and when the call came, I said I'd go. Two other seamen also volunteered for the job.

As I stood there looking into "CL" compartment, my companion, a seaman named "Smitty," called to me. I turned to see him on the opposite side of the conveyor trying to help a shipmate whose back was against the bulkhead, but who was slowly slipping to the deck (floor). His eyes were rolled back into his head. He looked like he was dying.

"This one is still alive," Smitty said calmly. Smitty was a small fellow but he managed to wrestle the wounded shipmate to me and I pulled his limp body over the conveyor into the passageway. If on December 6th anyone had asked me to help save the life of this offensive guy, I would have answered, "To hell with him." I had known this fellow since boot-camp, and he was one of the most overbearing individuals I had ever met. But now, unconscious, he had no personality; his was a life to be saved.

To reach the first-aid station, Smitty and I back-tracked aft on the starboard side. Now and then, we had to stop and lay him down, so we could rest. Catching our breaths, we moved on again. As we trudged along, we had to again open and close the watertight bulkhead doors while making our way back through the passageway to a ladder up, which was near the man-hole down to number three lower handling, from where we started. The hatch-cover at the top of the ladder was dogged down—another Navy term for closed and watertight. But, it was the nearest escape to the decks above. We undogged the hatch and pushed it open. Smitty took the injured man's legs and started up the ladder; I got him under the arms again and just as I'd taken a second or third step up the ladder an explosion again rocked the ship.

Sorting the Living from the Dead

Suddenly, a steam pipe nearby blew out. In a stunning moment of chaos that followed, I heard the cry, "Gas!" Unquestioningly, I held my breath until I could fit my gas mask to my face. The gas mask was very uncomfortable and it was difficult to cope with. Finally, I lifted it a bit to sniff the air to determine whether or not it smelled safe to breathe; it did.

Smitty and I debated whether to try to escape by going back to "CL" compartment and try a ladder there, or opening this hatch again and trying to escape here. Hesitatingly, we again tackled this ladder. We again opened the hatch cover and saw no evidence of damage from the explosion.

What actually happened was a bomb penetrated the decks above and exploded in front of the ship's store, several feet forward of the ladder. It killed "Boots," one of the masters-at-arms (ship's policeman). It bent a heavy steel hatch-combing flush with the deck.

We picked up our injured shipmate and carried him up. This time, we were lucky and got him to the first-aid station.

Some station! It was normally the crews' recreation room, but now a state of incredible confusion prevailed. We laid our shipmate on the deck. A chief petty officer, whom I recognized as one of the "black-gang" (engine room crew), came over and with great authority asked if he was alive. "We think so," I said. "Then get him out of the way," ordered the chief. "Slide him under the table where nobody will trip over him." (Later in the week, I learned that the fellow's back had been broken, but he would recover.) Then the chief went back to directing and sorting the living from the dead. As men brought in casualties, the chief would say, "Dead or alive? If they're dead, take them into the other room and throw them on the dead pile." He repeatedly made rounds of the room inspecting bodies. "This man is dead— Get him out of here." Normally this cold, hard manner would have been resented. Now, I could only feel admiration for his efficiency.

Abandon Ship

As I stood, trying to comprehend all of this, someone handed me a bottle of rootbeer and a sandwich. Ordinarily I would have retched at the sight of so much blood, but I ate and drank, completely amazed at my appetite under such conditions and decided it was all incomprehensible.

While I was in the first-aid station, word came to abandon ship. Whether or not this was an official order, I don't know. But instead, the Chief Petty Officer in charge, and a Warrant Officer, named Applegate, formed a work-party of ten men to search for anti-aircraft ammunition, since ours could not be reached, due to a bomb explosion.

Our work-party first went aft to the door which exited onto the starboard quarter-deck. We were about to proceed across the quarter-deck to board a motor launch when someone warned us that a wave of strafing Japanese planes was passing over. The planes came in low, firing their machine guns. Between sorties, men from nearby battle stations raced out on the quarterdeck and dragged to shelter those who had been struck by the machine gun fire. Then, as soon as we felt it was safe, we ran for the motor launch, which was waiting for us at the port quarter, dry docks. She seemed to be out of the channel, perhaps she had turned to avoid a bomb.

Our coxswain took our launch into the space between the capsized *Oklahoma* and the port side forecastle of the *Maryland*. Shouting up to sailors on the *Maryland*'s forecastle, we tried to convey to them that we needed ammunition, but we could rouse no support. Their problems were far greater to them than what we were shouting up to them from our motor launch. . . .

Brush with a Giant Propeller

Once it became clear that we could expect no help from this quarter, we gave up trying to board the *Maryland*. The coxswain maneuvered the motor launch from between the two battleships and motored around the whale shaped hull of the capsized *Oklahoma* and went to the USS *West Virginia*.

By this time, the *West Virginia* had sunk deep enough so that it was with little effort that Warrant Officer Applegate, and the five men he picked, to clamber aboard. I watched as they crossed the ship's forecastle, walking under the barrels of the 16-inch guns, and walk aft on the starboard side. We never saw them again.

Within minutes the forecastle shot up in smoke and flames. (It may have been the bomb that hit the turret of the *Tennessee.*) An officer in his white uniform appeared engulfed in the fire. Someone on board shouted, "Get out of there. The ship can blow up any minute."

The explosion frightened us terribly. The coxswain began backing the launch away from the burning battleship, Suddenly, I saw that the coxswain was not aware of the danger immediately behind our launch; we were backing straight for one of the large propellers of the capsized *Oklahoma* sticking high out of the water.

I yelled at the coxswain, "Reverse your engines." At the same time, two of us clambered to the tiller-deck, and scrambled over the taffrail. With one hand grasping the taffrail, we reached with our legs—spread eagle like—and with our feet, shoved against the propeller. Unquestionably, our effort prevented the motor launch from being damaged; but we just did what the situation required.

The coxswain now had the launch underway forward. Then we saw a man struggling in the water near the midships section of the *West Virginia.* "We're going in after him," he told us. The coxswain maneuvered in to pick up the man from the water, bringing him dangerously close to the perimeter of the burning oil that was closing in.

By now I was overwhelmed by all that was happening around us and for the life of me, I can't recall whether that man made it into the boat. We headed for 1010 dock at the Navy shipyard.

No Words to Describe It

And there was, indeed, reason to feel overwhelmed. On every side were almost unbearable sights. Battleship Row was devastated. From the direction of the dry docks, an explosion shook the harbor. This was the destroyer *Shaw.* Just two weeks before, I had visited my brother's ship in that same dry dock.

The *St. Louis* was gaining speed, but we were able to come alongside her starboard quarter . . . where we tried to clamber aboard the gangway which was still hanging over the side. An officer on deck denied us permission to come aboard. Frustrated, we abandoned the attempt to board the *St. Louis* and headed for 1010 dock at the Naval Ship Yard, where everyone went their individual ways.

Only one who was there can fully appreciate what took place. As a Pearl Harbor survivor who was at ground zero on "Battleship Row," the morning of December 7, 1941, I feel, "if you didn't go through it, there's no words that can adequately describe it; if you were there, then no words are necessary."

Fire on the Waters

Bill Steedly

> Although all the ships in Battleship Row were vulnerable and
> many suffered terrible damage, the USS *Vestal* turned out to
> be in a particularly dangerous spot—right alongside the USS
> *Arizona*. The *Vestal* ended up taking numerous hits intended
> for the much larger *Arizona*, and when the fatal bomb struck
> the latter, the explosion blew the men standing on the *Vestal*'s
> decks into the water. There, many experienced a horrendous
> ordeal as they fought to keep from drowning as well as being
> burned to death by the oil fires that raged on the water's sur-
> face. Chief Petty Officer Bill Steedly, whose testimony fol-
> lows, was one of the lucky ones who escaped and lived to tell
> the tale.

On the morning of 7 December, I got out of my bunk in
the chief petty officers' quarters and went to the wash-
room. I had already shaved and was under the shower when
I heard a tremendous blast. Our ship lurched up, and I lost
my footing and fell in the shower room. I learned later that
we had a bomb hit in the crew's mess hall. I ran to my
clothes locker and hurriedly put on my clothes. General
quarters was sounding to man the battle stations. Then we
took another bomb hit in the compartment forward of the
chief petty officers' quarters, where I had been a few minutes earlier. After that hit, we took another bomb hit in the
carpenter shop. This bomb went through the carpenter shop,
then through an oil tank and out the bottom of the ship. A
chief storekeeper and I were the last ones to get up the lad-

Excerpted from *Eyewitness to Infamy: An Oral History of Pearl Harbor, December 7,
1941*, edited by Paul Travers (New York: Madison, 1991).

der from below. The reason was that we were also hit by incendiary bombs. There was a fire blocking our only exit. We tried to go forward, but all we could see was water leaking around the door. We looked through the glass built into the door, and we could see that the compartment was almost completely flooded. We tightened the dogs (latches) holding the door and at the same time heard the word passed to abandon ship. At that time I learned that our captain had been blown overboard. After about twenty-five minutes of waiting for the fire to cool down, we started up the exit ladder again. I ran to the side of the ship as quick as I could and dove into the water. I didn't remember seeing anything but fire and smoke when I finally made it on deck. The water was kind of a rude awakening. But after being stuck below deck in the middle of a fire, it felt refreshing.

A Wall of Fire

Then all of a sudden, we had fire on the water between the stern of the *Vestal* and the battleship *Maryland*. We quickly realized we were swimming in a sea of gasoline and of oil from the ruptured fuel tanks. All at once, the fire blazed up and burned the shirt off my back. A lot of men were swimming around in the water, screaming and hollering for help. It was a sad sight to see those men who were struggling in the water disappear in a wall of fire that completely surrounded them. They tried to move away from the fire, but couldn't get away in time. The burning oil and burning flesh made a sickening, hard-to-describe smell. After my shirt was burned off, I swam out of the fire and saw a piece of timber floating by. I swam over and got my arm around it and, with the other arm, paddled away from the burning oil which covered the water next to the ships. Now that we were away from the ships, we had a little better view of what was going on. Even then it was hard to make out what was happening to the battleships. Everything was surrounded by smoke and fire, and by now gun crews had opened up on the Jap planes and filled the sky with black bursts. In the meantime, the Japs were coming in again, dropping their torpedoes and strafing

us in the water. The water turned to dots of red when one of
the men got hit by the machine-gun fire. Most of us were like
ducks on the pond. When we tried to move away from where
we thought the bullets were going to strike, it was like we
were moving in slow motion in a dream. At one time, I was
thinking what would happen to me if I got hit by one of the
Jap torpedoes. It was as if, with the fire and the machine
guns, I didn't have enough to worry about.

Abandon Ship Again

I can't remember how long we stayed in the water, but it
seemed like hours. After the last attack, our captain swam
back to the gangway and called for us to come aboard. A lot
of us went back and, once aboard, cut the Manila lines that
weren't already burned, so that we could get underway. The
ship got underway, and, the way we were riding in the water, it looked like we were going to sink at any minute. Our
captain ran the ship aground at Aiea Shoal. The Japs started
strafing us again, so our captain had us abandon ship once
again. This time we ended up in a cane field a short way
from the ship.

Our captain was Commander Cassin C. Young. He was
later made four stripes and given the Congressional Medal
of Honor by Admiral Chester Nimitz. After the attack, we
worked on our ship and at the same time worked on other
combat ships. While we were making a patch for the hole in
the carpenter ship, we pumped out the compartments
flooded by the other bombs. We were one of the last ships
to go into dry dock. We were still in Pearl Harbor during the
Battle of Midway. Approximately eleven months later in the
South Pacific battle area, while repairing damaged ships, we
went alongside the USS *San Francisco*. We found out that
Commander Young had been killed in a night engagement
with the Jap fleet. His ship was shot all to pieces and all the
officers were killed, I was told.

Caught in the Second Wave of Attackers

Ephraim P. Holmes

Lieutenant (later Admiral) Ephraim P. Holmes was a staff commander of battleships at the time of the Pearl Harbor attack. When the first wave of Japanese planes began bombing, he was far from the harbor and unable to reach the scene until the first attack was already over. His account, which follows, is notable for its precise, accurate descriptions of the damaged ships, the onset of the second wave of enemy planes, efforts by sailors aboard the USS *Maryland* to fight back, and the attempts by several vessels to extinguish raging fires in Battleship Row following the departure of the second wave.

E arly in the morning of December 7, 1941, I was proceeding with Lieut. Comdr. (MC) A.C. Hohn enroute to Fort Shafter. We observed the sky in the general location of Pearl Harbor to be filled with bursts and heard heavy firing.

We decided to proceed to Pearl Harbor and to go to our ship. Enroute we observed the firing to continue and at one point saw a great explosion in or near Pearl Harbor which we thought to be an oil tank explosion, but which we have come subsequently to believe to have been the explosion of the *Arizona*.

The Second Attack Begins

I saw numerous groups of airplanes in the sky, but have no knowledge of their identity or number. I noted at this time

Excerpted from *Pearl Harbor: Why, How, Fleet Salvage, and Final Appraisal*, by Homer N. Wallin (Washington, DC: Naval History Division, 1968).

that there was considerable cloud-cover over most of Pearl; otherwise clear.

When we arrived in the Yard the first attack was over. I ran to the Officers' Club Landing; Lieut. Comdr. Hohn stopped near the Fleet Landing to attend to some injured men who were just beginning to get ashore. At the Landing I saw the *Oklahoma* had turned over. Great fires on the surface of the water were burning near the *West Virginia* and *Arizona*, completely obscuring the latter. The *West Virginia* was already settling low in the water. I jumped in the first boat available, *ComDesRon One* gig, with a junior officer from the *California;* left him at the *California* (he stepped from the boat to the Main Deck of the *California*); and proceeded to the *Maryland*, arriving at about 0840–0850. A lull in the attack occurred at this time and when I boarded the *Maryland*. I went to my room to put on some shoes and get binoculars, Signal Book and revolver. While there another attack started. As soon as I could get out (Main Deck hatches were closed at this time), I proceeded to the Signal Bridge, passing over the Boat Deck. Somewhere enroute I felt a considerable shock which I thought a near miss. In passing across the Boat Deck I noted a large number of empty cartridge cases. All hands at the guns seemed to be very tense but collected and determined.

I remained on the Signal Bridge the rest of the day. Much intermittent firing occurred and several groups of Japanese planes were sighted and fired at. The planes observed were single-wing, single-motored types of moderate speed, probably not over 200 m.p.h. at the most. I saw but one that gave evidence of being hit in the air. It was over the location of Hickam Field; broke into smoke and appeared to be in difficulty but I did not see it crash.

When the Commander-in-Chief, Pacific Fleet order was received not to sortie our bridge passed it by visual [that is, by signal flags] to the *Phoenix*, *Raleigh*, and *Detroit* who were underway. When later the order was intercepted for all cruisers and destroyers to sortie we made a hoist to all cruisers and destroyers to sortie indicating the originator as the Commander-in-Chief, Pacific Fleet.

Fighting Raging Fires

When the fire was raging in and alongside the *West Virginia*, *YG17* promptly and without orders put its bow into the fire and pumped water onto it for hours. The *Tern* and *Widgeon* were ordered by Commander Battleships to assist. Their able work eventually checked the fire. At one point in this fire fighting episode a motor whale boat from the *Honolulu* expended CO_2 extinguishers in the fire by the *West Virginia* by making repeated runs along the edge of the fire. Each time this was done the sides of the boat broke into flames, which had to be put out before the next run. The heat was so intense that the men in the boat had to lean way over the unexposed side to protect themselves.

The *Maryland* delivered a heavy AA fire from all AA batteries on each occasion of opening up. The 1.1 mounts near the Signal Bridge functioned very well. It is believed, however, that both these guns and the .50 cal. machine guns had a tendency to open fire at too great ranges. This was caused, no doubt, by eagerness to engage the enemy but should be guarded against in the future.

After the *West Virginia* fire had been brought under control, *YG17* and the *Tern* were directed to shift their efforts to the fire burning in the *Arizona*. This was done in the forenoon of December 8. During that same day the *Navajo* reported to Commander Battleships for orders. After determining that the *California* did not need her services she was likewise ordered to assist in fighting the fire in the *Arizona*.

Chapter 3

Land Targets and Installations

Chapter Preface

The harbor was not the only area on Oahu targeted by Fuchida and his pilots. The Hickam, Wheeler, and Bellows airfields came under attack, too, as the Japanese attempted to destroy local American airpower while it was still on the ground. This goal was largely achieved, although a handful of American pilots did manage to get their planes into the air and shoot down a few enemy craft.

At Hickam Field, the large, new consolidated barracks was one of the main targets. The engineering building was devastated, as were Hangars 11 and 15; several other hangars sustained moderate or minor damage. Because the planes on the runway were parked so close together, when one was hit the explosion often ignited the others around it. Luckily, the attackers failed to find and destroy the base's underground fuel tanks; they mistakenly thought they were under the baseball field, which was gutted by bombs. Meanwhile, airmen set up defensive machine-gun nests wherever they could— sometimes right in the open—and blazed away at the incoming planes. There were not enough machine guns to go around. So some of the men used ordinary rifles and even handguns in a desperate attempt to fend off the attackers.

Wheeler Field suffered similar devastation. Several hangars were nearly obliterated, including Hangar 1; fortunately, though, the structure's back wall, made of cement blocks, held and thereby protected several engineering shops from destruction. Not so lucky was the barracks of the Sixth Pursuit Squadron, which took a severe hit. At the same time, a number of enlisted men died when Japanese planes flew low and strafed a row of tents where the men had been quartered.

Besides airplanes, hangars, and barracks, the Japanese targeted houses and other living quarters on the bases. Those that were not bombed were strafed with machine-gun fire. The hospital south of Pearl Harbor was also strafed, as were soldiers stationed at Fort Kamehameha (near the mouth of the harbor) and other defensive installations. People running along the ground, military personnel and civilians alike, also became targets.

The Devastation at Hickam Field

Ginger, a High School Senior

> Following is an entry from the diary of a high school senior, Ginger (whose last name is withheld at her request). At the time of the attack on Oahu she was living with her parents and attending school at Hickam Field. Her account gives a riveting and useful general view of the assault on the air base, including a list of the major buildings destroyed or damaged.

S unday, December 7, 1941
   BOMBED! 8:00 in the morning. Unkown attacker so far! Pearl Harbor in flames! Also Hickam hangar line. So far no houses bombed here.

   5 of 11:00. We've left the post. It got too hot. The PX [military store] is in flames, also the barracks. We made a dash during a lull. Left everything we own there. Found out the attackers are Japs. Rats!!! A couple of non-com's [non-commissioned officers] houses demolished. Hope Kay is O.K. We're at M's. It's all so sudden and surprising I can't believe it's really happening. It's awful. School is discontinued until further notice . . . there goes my graduation. . . .

Fireworks at Hickam

The following was typed on a separate place of paper attached to the diary page:

   I was awakened at eight o'clock on the morning of December 7th by an explosion from Pearl Harbor. I got up

---

Excerpted from "Ginger's Diary," www.essentialpearlharbor.com, December 7, 1941.

thinking something exciting was probably going on over there. Little did I know! When I reached the kitchen the whole family, excluding Pop, was looking over at the Navy Yard. It was being consumed by black smoke and more terrific explosions. We didn't know what was going on, but I didn't like it because the first explosion looked as if it was right on top of Marie's house. I went and told Pop that (he in the meantime had gotten dressed and was leaving) and he said, "Who cares about Marie when you and Mom might be killed!" Then I became extremely worried, as did we all. Mom and I went out on the front porch to get a better look and three planes went zooming over our heads so close we could have touched them. They had red circles on their wings. Then we caught on! About that time bombs started dropping all over Hickam. We stayed at the windows, not knowing what else to do, and watched the fireworks. It was just like the news reels of Europe, only worse. We saw a bunch of soldiers come running full tilt towards us from the barracks and just then a whole line of bombs fell behind them knocking them all to the ground. We were deluged in a cloud of dust and had to run around closing all the windows. I got back to the front door just in time to see Pop calmly walking back to the house through it all. He said we could leave if a lull came. Also that a Mrs. B was coming down to our house and to wait for her. Then he left again. In the meantime a bunch of soldiers had come into our garage to hide. They were entirely taken by surprise and most of them didn't even have a gun or anything. One of them asked for a drink of water saying he was sick. He had just been so close to where a bomb fell that he had been showered with debris. He said he was scared, and I was too, so I couldn't say that I blamed him. I saw an officer out in the front yard, so Mom said to ask him if he thought it would be wise for us to try to leave. He said, "I would hate to say because we don't know whether they are bombing in town or not, and besides this is your home."

I no sooner got back into the house then a terrible barrage came down just over by the Post Exchange. That's just a block kitty corner from us, so the noise and concussion was terrific. Mom and I were still standing in the doorway and we saw the PX get hit. I was getting more worried by the minute about this time as they seemed to be closing in the circle they had been making around us. (The Japs were flying around in a circle bombing us, Pearl Harbor, and machine-gunning Fort Kam.) A second terrific bunch of explosions followed the first by a few minutes only. I found out later these had landed in the baseball diamond just a second after Dad had walked across it. He ran back to see if the men in a radio truck there had been hit. All but one had and they were carted off in an ambulance. I went dashing into my room to look and saw that the barracks was on fire, also the big depot hangar. I hated to go into my room because the planes kept machine-gunning the street just outside my window and I kept expecting to see a string of bullets come through my roof any minute. We had all gotten dressed in the meantime and had packed a suitcase and were ready to leave any time. Finally, after two and a half hours, the planes went away and we left. I gave the soldiers in the garage two and a half packages of my chewing gum before I left and they nearly died of joy at sight of it. Poor guys!!

Debris Everywhere

As we left the Post, we looked around to see what damage had been done to the place. The barracks was all on fire, the big depot was on fire, the theater was burned to the ground already, the PX was wrecked, the whole hangar line was blown up on the far side of Operations, a couple of the non-coms houses were very badly blown out, there was debris all over everywhere, and Pearl Harbor was just a solid wall of smoke which we found out later was burning oil from the boats that had been hit. Reports are that nothing was hit there except boats.

As we drove into town we found the highway blocked solid in all three lanes coming out to the Post as the radio had been calling for all personnel of the Army or Navy to return to their posts at once. We were forced to drive out in the gutter, and every now and then we had to move aside from there to let an ambulance go by. The people in town were standing along the street watching it all with very dazed looks. Of course, they didn't know what was going on as the radio hadn't said a thing about it. (We turned it on at home before we left and there amidst all the concussion and noise all we could get was church music.) We ran into Bill on the way into town and made him come back with us. (He had been at the University practicing shooting and had missed it all.)

A Hickam Airman Runs for His Life

Joseph A. Pesek

Technical Sergeant Joseph A. Pesek, of the U.S. Army Air Corps, was stationed with the 5th Bomber Group at Hickam Field at the time of the attack. In this exciting first-person account, he offers the useful perspective of one who ran across large sections of the base, chronicling the actions of many comrades while repeatedly escaping death himself at every turn.

On the morning of December 7, 1941, I got up shortly after 6 A.M. and walked to the NCO club for breakfast which was adjacent to the Pearl Harbor Naval Base. At the time I was a Tech Sergeant in the 5th Bomber Group and sharing half of a duplex government house with Joe Barrett, 4th Recon Squadron. After breakfast, I headed for the bus stop to wait for the 8:05 bus to take me to Honolulu where I was to play golf at the Wai Lai Golf Course.

While sitting there on a bench, I noticed a large flight of aircraft approaching from the northwest flying at an altitude of about 15,000 feet and at a distance which made identification impossible. I had seen similar flights come in preceding the arrival of U.S. aircraft carriers and just assumed another of our carriers was coming into port at Pearl Harbor. They approached at a point almost due north of where I was sitting and suddenly began to peal off in steep dives into the harbor. I watched a large torpedo-shaped bomb drop from the first plane followed by a huge explosion.

Death on the Parade Ground

As one after the other dropped their torpedoes, terrific explosions and flames were plainly visible. At the time, I thought it strange but possible that the Navy was conducting some sort of exercise and possibly destroying something over in the west locks where the target ship *Utah* and other old ships were moored. As the first plane pulled up only several hundred feet to my left with machine guns blazing, I saw the Rising Sun insignia on the wings and knew we were under attack.

He was flying over Hickam Air Field at an altitude of approximately 150 ft. A young boy was waiting at the bus stop with me and I told him to get home as fast as he could. By that time, clouds of black smoke were rising over the Harbor and planes were pulling up across Hickam toward the flight line with machine guns firing. When I got back to my quarters, Joe Barret was just getting up to see what all the noise was about. I yelled to him to move it as we were under attack.

After throwing on a pair of coveralls over my civies, we took off running toward the consolidated barracks and flight line. By this time, things were hectic and we had to hit the ground every few minutes due to low-flying strafing planes. As we were crossing the parade ground headed for the hangar line, we ran into Dave Jacobson and three other guys trying to set up an old WWI water-cooled machine gun and they were having problems with the tripod. Joe and I both had prior hitches in the Infantry so we had it assembled and in operational order quickly. I believe that had there not been a lull in the strafing, we would have stayed right there, but I guess it was not to be.

It wasn't long after we left that Dave and his crew took a direct hit that blew them to bits. The only way they identified Dave was by finding a section of his finger with his ring still in place. . . .

Hangar 7 Takes a Direct Hit

As we ran toward the hangar, we stayed close to the bar-racks so we wouldn't be out in the open as the planes were again overhead. There I saw another friend of mine, George Bolan lying face up, undoubtedly killed by concussion as there was no blood or signs of cuts that I could see. Yet his face was turning dark, possibly from broken blood vessels. When we got to the hangar, Joe went to his plane and I went into Hangar 7. They were passing out rifles from the arma-ment room so I got in line thinking at least it may be some protection later on. By the time I reached the head of the line, all rifles and helmets had been given out. I then started to carry canisters of 50 caliber ammo out of the armament room so they could be loaded into any of the aircraft still in commission. Several minutes later, I was returning for an-other canister when someone coming out said all the ammo was out, so I turned around and headed out the large sliding doors. Just then the hangar took a hit from a large bomb dropped from a high altitude flight. It felt as though the whole hangar was lifted from the ground. The next thing I knew, I was picking myself up off the ramp between Hangars 7 and 11, my back covered with white plaster blown out from the hangar.

Someone ran up to me and handed me a pint of whiskey. I took a gulp holding the bottle with both hands and al-though I don't remember being scared, my hands shook so much I almost dropped the bottle before giving it back. Next, I went to the adjacent Hangar 9 where Ed Caton, Freddie Lewis and JP Bock were. For a little while, there was another lull so we just sat and talked. I remember JP smoking a cigarette so fast it was like a fuse burning with a flame at the end of it.

A Hole in the Runway

In about 15 minutes, the planes were back and Ed and Fred-die were kneeling on the flight line side of the hangar, fir-ing at them as they flew along the row of hangars. Once they passed, I took off across the runway toward the John Rogers

Airport which was located where the present Honolulu International Airport is now. Before I got to the middle of the runway, I saw low-flying aircraft approaching from the east and I hit the ground again. While waiting for them to pass, someone hit the ground next to me and said, "Where are you headed, soldier?" I looked up and it was Brig. Gen. Jacob H. Rudolph, commander of the Eighteenth Bombardment Wing. I said, "I'm not sure where I'm going, but I know it's away from the hangars."

I got up and started to run again and almost made the edge of the runway when three more planes came at me. They were so low that I could see the ground kicking up where their machine-gun bullets were hitting. I hit the ground again, covering my head with my hands. It seemed as though a thousand things passed through my mind, mostly of home and my family. I could not believe it when those three planes passed right over without hitting me.

I looked up as they passed and thought the sky never looked bluer. I didn't even notice it at the time, but I tore my fingernails down until they were bleeding, trying to make a hole in the runway, I guess. Across the runway, I found a hole about 4 feet deep and 10 feet across which I dove into and, for the first time since the bombing began, I felt like I had made it. I was in the pit, which I learned later was dug for a base perimeter security exercise, for no more than five minutes when one of our large refueling trucks pulled up and stopped with one of his tires flat from being hit by one of the strafers. I could just picture another strafer hitting the truck and filling my hole with flaming fuel. I jumped from my security blanket and was out in the open again.

His House Demolished

Finally, the driver of the truck, who was a kid from my squadron, and I decided things were quieting down. He went back to the motor pool and had them bring out a huge jack and for at least the next hour, I helped him change the wheel. I then went back across the runway to the 5th Bomb. Group Personnel Office where a bunch of guys I knew had gathered. When Mike Kocan saw me, he said that he went by my quarters earlier and thought I had been killed. He told me that a small bomb hit up against the curb in front of my house and blew right through it. When I finally got back to my house (Tuesday P.M.) I found that my wrist watch, knocked from the top of my dresser into the open drawer, had the only piece of glass in the house that wasn't broken, including the tiles in the bathroom.

No one slept the night of December 7, 1941. I went over to the Operations Building and listened to reports coming in out from the command post that had been set up there. I have read many accounts and talked to a lot of eyewitnesses and survivors and stories differ. Many people were still in bed when the attack first began and saw things a little differently according to where they were at first sightings. One of the few who I know, who was also up and in a good spot to observe things was my Group Commanding Officer, General Farthing. He and I traded experiences later and our stories as to what we saw and what took place in those first few minutes were exactly the same.

Assaults on Living Quarters

Stephen and Flora Belle Koran

Stephen Koran was an Air Corps aerial photographer assigned to Oahu in 1939. He, his wife Flora Belle, and their infant daughter lived at Wheeler Field in a two-bedroom duplex located about a thousand yards from the photography lab where he worked. They were at home that Sunday morning when the first wave of Japanese planes attacked, and their ordeal, as they tell it below, constitutes an example of numerous instances when the attackers strafed personnel quarters as well as military targets. Stephen's literate and detailed account is also valuable for its descriptions of the bombing of the planes at Wheeler Field and the successful attempt of a handful of Wheeler pilots to get into the air and fight back.

Stephen: "We heard the aircraft coming in. We didn't give it too much thought because, prior to the December attack, what the Air Corps used to do is periodically go over unannounced on a Sunday morning and put a mock raid on Pearl Harbor to see how fast the Navy could get up, get out of bed, and get their aircraft in the air. It wasn't on any schedule. Maybe two or three weeks later, the Navy would do the same thing to us. Of course, we didn't know which week it would be because it wasn't supposed to be run on a scheduled basis. It so happened that, just a couple of weeks prior to December 7, we had done our buzz job on the Navy, and it was their turn to do it to us.

Excerpted from *Remembering Pearl Harbor: Eyewitness Accounts by U.S. Military Men and Women*, edited by Robert S. La Forte and Ronald E. Marcello (Wilmington, DE: Scholarly Resources, 1991).

So we gave it no thought. I thought it was the Navy coming over, and I wasn't scheduled for any duty on the flight line, so I just laid there, and then I heard one plane that seemed like it pulled out and went into a screeching dive. I mentioned to my wife that 'if he doesn't pull out of it, he's going to crash.' I no sooner got the word *crash* out of my mouth than I heard a great big explosion. Well, I was in such a position that I leaned on my elbow on the bed and looked out of my window. I could see the engineering hangar off in the distance. I saw black smoke coming out of it, and I remarked: 'My gosh, he's crashed into the engineering hangar!'

All Hell Broke Loose

About that time I saw another plane pull out, and I saw a little black object drop down. When he dropped the object he pulled up, and that's when I noticed the red disk around the aircraft. I yelled to my wife: 'Let's get out of here! It's the Japs! It's not the Navy!' Then all hell broke loose.

Our quarters were built of cinder blocks, with stucco on the outside, and the inner walls were also cinder block. So my first thought was to get my family into the inner room, away from the bombs. This was all well and good until in the course of the bombing they must have dropped a bomb in the rear of the quadrangle where we lived, and a back window frame in our back bedroom blew out.

When that happened, I figured that this was no place for us to be. I remembered that up the street, a block from us, there was a great big banyan tree. Underneath this banyan tree there was an abandoned cesspool which we knew was dry. My main object was to try to get my family out of the house and down into this abandoned cesspool.

So my wife grabbed the baby, and we started out of the house. There were a couple of other couples running down the street, heading for the same place. About that time, I heard a plane coming pretty close. I managed to stick my head out from under the porch's roof, and I could see he was coming right down on the quarters. Evidently, he saw these people running down the street, and he was going for them.

When he started getting real close, I gave my wife a shove. She had the baby, and she landed down on the street by the curb. I took a flying leap on top of her. Just as I did that, he started machine-gunning into the roof of the porch that we had been underneath. As a matter of fact, she got dust in her eyes from the machine-gun bullets. They were that close to us as they went down the line.

We finally got back up again and headed down the block. My main object was to get them out of the house because, after the Japanese got through bombing the flight line and had done all the damage they could down there, they started to work on some of the quarters. When they started bombing and strafing the quarters, I knew that was no place for us."

Flora Belle: "It seemed like there was a bomb dropping every five seconds. My first thought was the baby lying in the bassinet. I thought: 'Oh, my, she's going to have her eardrums punctured!' I grabbed a down comforter and threw it double over the bassinet, and, when my husband said: 'It's the Japs! Get your clothes on!' I started to dress. In between grabbing things to dress, I thought: 'Oh, my goodness, what if they've poisoned the water!' It's very peculiar what you think of at a time like that. I must have had an arsenic bomb in mind. I had read someplace where that had been done.

While I was dressing, there was a young man outside our house hugging the wall right next to the window. I rushed over and screamed out the window: 'Come in out of sight!' I screamed and screamed, and he absolutely did not hear me because the din was so loud.

There was a little pause after the first wave went over. We went across the street to Shorty and Marge. Shorty was laughing to beat the band. You think of some funny things. During the middle of the bombing, Marge was dancing up and down and clapping her hands, having a conniption fit, saying: 'Oh, what'll I wear, what'll I wear?' She had dozens of things in the closet.

But then a second wave came over, and we made it to the cesspool. There were about three high-test gasoline trucks that they had brought in there, and they parked them so that there would be some fuel left if the main supplies got blown up. So we—Marge, the baby and I, and her little Scottie dog—squeezed ourselves into a space about 3 feet by 4 feet and about 2 feet sunken under the ground. It was concrete lined but open at the top.

We were under the banyan tree, and the trucks were parked there because banyan trees are so thick that from the air you cannot spot things underneath them. If one tracer bullet had hit those . . . I didn't think about it at the time."

Stephen: "Between the first and second attacks there was a little incident that happened that irritated me quite a bit. I think, if they wanted to, they could have court-martialed me.

The boys were gathering around one of the hangars which was our ordnance depot, and all the machine guns were behind the fenced-in area back of the hangar. A young second lieutenant, a shavetail, was the ordnance officer, and the boys were trying to get the machine guns out, but he refused to give the guns up because they did not have a damned requisition. Well, I came down there, and, being one of the senior noncoms, they came over and told me about it. So I went in there, and the lieutenant started to give me some guff, and I pulled out my .45 and told him: 'Lieutenant, if you don't open up that damned cage, I'm going to put one right between your eyes,' and he opened the cage, and we got the guns out.

The way I looked at it, if you've got bombs falling around you and people getting killed, and you see a bunch of guns, the first initiative of any normal human being is to grab one and see what he could do. It just irritated me to see some young lieutenant guarding the damned thing with all the guns back there and saying: 'You can't have them because you don't have an order to get them.'

Launching a Counterattack

When the second attack began there were an awful lot of bombs blowing up around the place. I got down to the flight line, and I could see all these aircraft. Their nose and tail would be sticking up, because the incendiary bullets had gotten right down the middle and had burned out the center of the aircraft. Of a total of all aircraft we had out there, we had 120 that were burned up on the field. They were all pursuit ships. Bear in mind, the Japanese hit our base first, before they hit Pearl Harbor, because we had the fighter aircraft.

But fortunately we had one of our squadrons that happened to be at Haleiwa, on the north shore, having gunnery practice. Of course, that Saturday there was a party going on at the club. We had Lieutenant George S. Welch, who was a youngster at that time, Lieutenant Kenneth M. Taylor, and Lieutenant Philip M. Rasmussen, who happened to be living in the BOQ [bachelor officers' quarters] there. They were still half asleep and still had their tuxedos on from the previous party.

Lieutenant Taylor had a little MG. When the first bomb dropped, they jumped into that MG and went the eleven miles from Wheeler Field to Haleiwa, where their airplanes were parked underneath trees. They traveled that eleven miles in less than six minutes. While this was going on, their crew chiefs had loaded their P-40s, and, when they got there, they jumped into their aircraft while they were still in their tuxedos, and they got down the sand runway and were airborne. In order to get airborne, Lieutenant Welch had to waggle his wings to knock the ammunition boxes off each wing. Welch landed and took off at least three times and during the process managed to shoot down five Japanese. I think Taylor got three, and Rasmussen, two.

I knew all of them well because they all had to report down to the photographic laboratory to take their official portraits. I got acquainted with Lieutenant Welch there, and we did a lot of work together before the war. I jokingly asked him, when he first came down there, when was the last time he shaved. He looked like he had just a little peach fuzz on his cheeks. He was one of the type of boys that nobody cared to fly with in formation. He was a poor formation flyer, but you could put him in a P-40 and let him fly by himself, and he'd turn that P-40 upside down, inside out, turn on a dime, and give you nine cents change to boot.

We had to make confirmation of the planes shot down. The reason we were able to officially certify this is that, when they have gunnery practice, they have the machine-gun cameras attached to the aircraft at the same time. So the cameras were automatically turned on when the machine guns started to fire, and they automatically started to take photographs. After the film was sent down, and the file was processed, we had official confirmation from all the aerial machine-gun film. There's where we got the official confirmation.

A Downed Enemy Plane

During the attack on Wheeler Field proper, there were a few planes shot down that crashed in the pineapple fields. One of our machine guns on top of the barracks managed to get one. After the bombing was all over, and things settled down, I was sent out to the pineapple field to locate this crashed Japanese plane and photograph it. It was a twin-

Wheeler Under Attack

Amplifying Stephen Koran's account of the attack on Wheeler Field is this overview of the devastation the base suffered, later pieced together by Air Force historian Leatrice R. Arakaki.

The Japanese hit Wheeler in two waves, the first shortly before 0800 and the second about an hour later. Principal targets of the first attack were aircraft and buildings along the hangar line and people in the immediate area. In the second raid, seven enemy planes approached from the south and fired machine guns at aircraft being taxied onto the airdrome. This attack, which lasted less than five minutes, was made by fighters and horizontal bombers expending the remainder of their ammunition after attacking the Kaneohe Naval Air Station. Wheeler had little protection against aerial attack, with no antiaircraft guns, no trenches, and no air raid shelters. The base had only five machine guns, which were mounted on top of the hangars and the big barracks; and the perimeter guard was armed with rifles.

engine, torpedo-type aircraft that they used as a dive-bomber. There were two bodies still in the aircraft—the pilot and the observer. They were burned pretty well beyond recognition. The one in the rear cockpit was leaning over with his arm sticking out of the side of the cockpit, and I noticed something peculiar that was on his hand. So I took a photograph of that hand with infrared film that I had. I also took photographs of the engine. When I processed these photographs, I blew up his hand to a 20-by-24 size, and we discovered that the ring that he was wearing happened to be that of a graduate of the Punahou High School, which was one of the high schools in Honolulu.

Another thing that struck me and made me all the more angrier and teed off was the fact that, after we blew up the prop, the manufacturer's plate on it, believe it or not, happened to be of an American engine they were using in a dive-bomber. It was a Hamilton-Standard prop. This was some of the air-

Colonel Flood, the base commander, was in front of his quarters talking to some people when the attack began. He saw a bomb hit near the Wheeler depot area and at first thought someone out on maneuvers must have accidentally dropped it. Immediately afterward, a group of low-flying airplanes sped by, only 50 to 75 feet off the ground. "You could almost hit them with a rock if you had it," thought Flood. When he saw the insignia of the Japanese rising sun, he knew what had happened and hurried down to the flight line. By then, hangars and aircraft were in flames, and a thick pall of black smoke hung over the area.

The bombs struck and burned Hangars 1 and 3, in addition to wrecking a PX storehouse and a warehouse filled with cement. One bomb hit the 6th Pursuit Squadron's barracks, entering a window on the second floor, where it exploded and caused considerable property damage and personal injuries. Another landed in an open area and made a crater 15 feet in diameter and 6 feet deep.

Leatrice R. Arakaki and John R. Kuborn, *7 December 1941: The Air Force Story.* Hickam Air Force Base, HI: Pacific Air Forces Office of History, 1991, p.111.

craft equipment and iron and stuff that we had sent over to Japan prior to the attack. This burned me up a bit more.

During the attack, I grabbed my camera. It just came as second nature. I figured I couldn't do anything else, so I thought I might as well try and get some sort of record of the attack. I photographed all the various flight lines—the ships that were burned out right in a beautiful row. I photographed the damaged hangars and took some general photographs showing the overall damage to the field proper.

I was photographing one particular area, and I saw one of the fellows running out for one aircraft that was still on the flight line that hadn't been damaged. Before he got there, the Japs got him. They dropped another bomb, and the concussion knocked me against the flight hangar. The reason I know this is because I unconsciously held the shutter trigger on, on the motion-picture camera I had. When we processed the film, that particular film showed the sky and the top of the hangar. After that bomb, all I found of him was his undershirt in a big hole out there, that's all.

After the second bombing was all over, everybody got as much armament and ammunition as they could get in their arms. They had a slight rumor that paratroopers had landed on the island of Oahu and that they were dressed in blue coveralls. Well, in those days the military had blue coveralls. So an order was issued that everybody in blue coveralls was to get out of them—wear anything, but get rid of the blue coveralls.

We had a perimeter set up at that time. After that things kind of settled down a bit. I went back to find out how my wife and daughter were doing, and she laughed when she saw me, because I figured, if something was going to happen, I was going to be prepared. I had taken about four bandoliers of .30-caliber shells wrapped crisscross across my chest. I had a Springfield rifle across my shoulder. I had a .45 on my hip, and I had about half-dozen grenades attached around me, and I was carrying a Thompson submachine gun in my left hand, and I had a steel helmet and gas mask on. I don't think I could have run a hundred feet if I had tried."

The Fight to Save the Injured

Ruth Erickson

> Even as the attack continued and Japanese planes strafed the
> areas around the hospitals, doctors and nurses in those build-
> ings struggled heroically to care for the enormous number of
> wounded. Throughout the morning, casualties, including
> many burn victims, streamed in from all directions. Lt. Ruth
> Erickson, a nurse at the Naval Hospital, located south of Pearl
> Harbor, gave this account of the fight to save the injured.

We had vacated the nurses' quarters about 1 week prior
to the attack. We lived in temporary quarters directly
across the street from the hospital, a one-story building in
the shape of an E. The permanent nurses' quarters had been
stripped and the shell of the building was to be razed in the
next few days.

By now, the nursing staff had been increased to 30 and an
appropriate number of doctors and corpsmen had been
added. The Pacific Fleet had moved their base of operations
from San Diego to Pearl Harbor. With this massive expansion, there went our tropical hours! The hospital now operated at full capacity. . . .

I had worked the afternoon duty on Saturday, December
6th from 3 P.M. until 10 P.M. with Sunday to be my day off.

Two or three of us were sitting in the dining room Sunday morning having a late breakfast and talking over coffee.
Suddenly we heard planes roaring overhead and we said,

"The 'fly boys' are really busy at Ford Island this morning." The island was directly across the channel from the hospital. We didn't think too much about it since the reserves were often there for weekend training. We no sooner got those words out when we started to hear noises that were foreign to us.

I leaped out of my chair and dashed to the nearest window in the corridor. Right then there was a plane flying directly over the top of our quarters, a one-story structure. The rising sun under the wing of the plane denoted the enemy. Had I known the pilot, one could almost see his features around his goggles. He was obviously saving his ammunition for the ships. Just down the row, all the ships were sitting there—the [battleships] *California* (BB-44), the *Arizona* (BB-39), the *Oklahoma* (BB-37), and others.

My heart was racing, the telephone was ringing, the chief nurse, Gertrude Arnest, was saying, "Girls, get into your uniforms at once. This is the real thing!"

I was in my room by that time changing into uniform. It was getting dusky, almost like evening. Smoke was rising from burning ships.

An Unending Stream of Burn Patients

I dashed across the street, through a shrapnel shower, got into the lanai and just stood still for a second as were a couple of doctors. I felt like I were frozen to the ground, but it was only a split second. I ran to the orthopedic dressing room but it was locked. A corpsmen ran to the OD's [Officer-of-the-Day's] desk for the keys. It seemed like an eternity before he returned and the room was opened. We drew water into every container we could find and set up the instrument boiler. Fortunately, we still had electricity and water. Dr. [CDR Clyde W.] Brunson, the chief of medicine, was making sick call when the bombing started. When he was finished, he was to play golf . . . a phrase never to be uttered again.

The first patient came into our dressing room at 8:25 A.M. with a large opening in his abdomen and bleeding profusely. They started an intravenous and transfusion. I can still see the tremor of Dr. Brunson's hand as he picked up the needle. Everyone was terrified. The patient died within the hour.

Then the burned patients streamed in. The USS *Nevada* (BB-36) had managed some steam and attempted to get out of the channel. They were unable to make it and went aground on Hospital Point right near the hospital. There was heavy oil on the water and the men dived off the ship and swam through these waters to Hospital Point, not too great a distance, but when one is burned . . . How they ever managed, I'll never know.

The tropical dress at the time was white t-shirts and shorts. The burns began where the pants ended. Bared arms and faces were plentiful.

Personnel retrieved a supply of flit guns from stock. We filled these with tannic acid to spray burned bodies. Then we gave these gravely injured patients sedatives for their intense pain.

Orthopedic patients were eased out of their beds with no time for linen changes as an unending stream of burn patients continued until mid afternoon. A doctor, who several days before had renal surgery and was still convalescing, got out of his bed and began to assist the other doctors. . . .

The Priest Was Busy

The laboratory was next to the tennis court. [A Japanese] plane sheared off a corner of the laboratory and a number of the laboratory animals, rats and guinea pigs, were destroyed, Dr. Shaver [LTJG John S.], the chief pathologist, was very upset.

About 12 noon the galley personnel came around with sandwiches and cold drinks; we ate on the run. About 2 o'clock the chief nurse was making rounds to check on all the units and arrange relief schedules.

I was relieved around 4 P.M. and went over to the nurses' quarters where everything was intact. I freshened up, had something to eat, and went back on duty at 8 P.M. I was scheduled to report to a surgical unit. By now it was dark and we worked with flashlights. The maintenance people and anyone else who could manage a hammer and nails were putting up black drapes or black paper to seal the crevices against any light that might stream to the outside.

About 10 or 11 o'clock, there were planes overhead. I really hadn't felt frightened until this particular time. My knees were knocking together and the patients were calling, "Nurse, nurse!" The other nurse and I went to them, held their hands a few moments, and then went onto others.

The priest was a very busy man. The noise ended very quickly and the word got around that these were our own planes.

I worked until midnight on that ward and then was directed to go down to the basement level in the main hospital building. Here the dependents—the women and children—the families of the doctors and other staff officers were placed for the night. There were ample blankets and pillows. We lay body by body along the walls of the basement. The children were frightened and the adults tense. It was not a very restful night for anyone.

Defending the Beaches

Roy Blick

> Oahu possessed several formidable coastal defenses, includ-
> ing Fort Kamehameha, on the coast southeast of Pearl Harbor
> and Hickam Field. Unfortunately, these installations were
> designed to repel an enemy attack on the beaches, and they
> were powerless to stop the Japanese warplanes that bombed
> the island. This informative eyewitness account of the attack
> as seen from an unusual vantage is by Roy Blick, then a pri-
> vate stationed at Fort Kamehameha.

I had a southern heritage, with both grandparents serving
in the Civil War with the Confederacy, an uncle who volunteered and lost his life in the Spanish-American War in
Cuba, and other relatives who served in World War I. I was
proud of those that had served and realized that we were
drawing closer to another war every day.

I had joined the Civil Conservation Corps in 1940 and
was stationed at Camp William Tell at Tell City, Indiana. On
3 February 1941, I left camp to go home to Lyon County,
Kentucky, for the weekend. I had an hour wait for another
bus in Evansville, so while I was waiting I took a walk that
delayed my trip to Kentucky and home for almost four
years. My walk took me past the post office, where I saw a
recruiting sign. I went in to talk with the recruiting sergeant
and enlisted for two years of overseas service as a replacement and was to get credit for a three-year enlistment. By

Excerpted from *Eyewitness to Infamy: An Oral History of Pearl Harbor, December 7,
1941*, edited by Paul Travers (New York: Madison, 1991).

11:00 P.M. I was in Fort Benjamin Harrison in Indianapolis, Indiana. By 6 February, I was in Fort Slocum, New York, to await overseas shipment. On 2 April, I left Fort Slocum for the Brooklyn Army and Navy Overseas Replacement Depot. On 8 April, I sailed on the USS *Washington* for Pearl Harbor, by way of the Panama Canal and San Francisco. On board we had twenty-five-hundred troops and a cargo of war bandages for the Chinese.

On 26 April, I arrived in Hawaii and went into training camp for six weeks. When the training was completed, I was assigned to A Battery, Fifteenth Coast Artillary, Fort Kamehameha, Territory of Hawaii, Pearl Harbor Defense. For a time, I was assigned to Fort Weaver, across the Pearl Harbor channel from Fort Kamehameha. By late summer, I had made the rating of first and fourth and was gun mechanic on the number-one sixteen-inch gun. I lived in the gun emplacement, with bunks in the toolshed.

The Woods Full of Smoke

On 7 December 1941, I awoke about 7:30 A.M. and was alone that morning at the sixteen-inch gun battery, except for the guards in the gun emplacement. One off-duty guard was asleep on an army cot under a tree, and the guard on duty was walking post and waiting for his relief, who had gone to chow. I told the guard that I would take his post if he wanted to go to chow before they threw everything out. He took me up on the other, and I took his post to wait for his relief.

It was a beautiful Sunday morning, with a good breeze. I was on the post only a few minutes when I heard a flight of planes coming in from the seaward side of our gun position. When the planes came over our position and flew over the Japanese salt beds into the harbor, they were very low and I could plainly see the Japanese pilots, and the large red circles under the wings were easy to identify. I called to Private Parsons, who was sleeping on the cot, that the Japanese were bombing the harbor. By this time, the guard had come back from chow, so I locked the gates to the gun position and divided the hundred rounds of ammo for the 1903

Springfields [rifles] that we were armed with. By now, the woods in Fort Weaver were full of smoke with shrapnel from the anti-aircraft fire and strafing planes. The gun crew was trying to make it to the gun position from the A Battery campsite near the marine barracks. The crew was using the woods for cover and yelling for me to open the gates. As I was moving toward the gate, a large object hit the sand nearby and sent a shower of sand and dust in the air. I hit the ground and waited, but whatever it was it didn't explode. I never went back to dig in the sand and find out what exactly it was.

The Invasion Never Came

When the gun crew made it to the gun emplacement, we took our battle stations. After someone shot the lock off of the magazine entrance, we were able to get out ammo by the case. We had plenty of targets and fired a lot of rounds, but we never knew if we hit anything. Being a gun mechanic, I had to check the pressure on the recoil cylinders and the re-cuperators on the sixteen-inch gun. We had by that time got-ten orders to be ready to fire, if we could get a target for the sixteen-inch gun. We never did get a target for the big gun, and we never fired a round from it during the attack. After checking the sixteen-inch gun, I took my position again, fir-ing my Springfield at passing Japanese planes. When a Japanese strafer ripped the sand within five feet of me, I took a position under the sixteen-inch gun that was de-pressed to about three feet off the ground. The gun finally found some use.

After the attack, we had no way of knowing what was next. From our position, we could see the smoke and fire in the harbor and hear explosions as they echoed across the water. We remained at our gun position for the day, and weeks and months following that. We dug trenches and built pillboxes by day and waited for the invasion by night. We had orders to defend the battery to the last man. The inva-sion never came, and in time the war moved across the Pa-cific. Most of us remained with the sixteen-inch guns, A

Battery Fifteenth Coast Artillery, for the defense of Pearl Harbor. We always remarked how fortunate we were that we never had to fire the sixteen-inch guns in actual defense of the harbor. If it ever did come to that, we knew we were in deep trouble and would most likely be fighting for our lives until the last man fell.

Chapter 4

The Immediate Aftermath

Chapter Preface

When the attackers finally headed back toward their ships around 10:00 A.M., the ordeal at Pearl Harbor was far from over. Thousands of men and women had been wounded, some of them severely, and in the hours following the disaster, they streamed into local hospitals, including the island's largest—Tripler Army Hospital, located several miles east of Pearl. As doctors and nurses tirelessly fought to save the wounded, armies of rescuers worked around the clock trying to free sailors trapped in the burning hulks of their once-proud ships. Thirty-two men were pulled from holes gouged in the upturned hull of the capsized *Oklahoma*, but many others from that vessel—448 to be exact—lost their lives.

Even while these desperate rescues continued, thousands of miles away in the United States, the country was in a state of shock. Standing before a packed joint session of Congress, President Roosevelt condemned the Japanese raid and called for war, which the legislators officially approved an hour later. Every group and faction in the country pulled together in the weeks that followed. And the mighty American military machine began to gear up and prepare to meet the coming challenge of total war.

Part of that challenge was replacing the crippled Pacific fleet. In perhaps the biggest salvage operation of the twentieth century, thousands of machines and mechanics raised the sunken ships (except for the *Arizona*, which became a sacred memorial), refloated them, and returned the majority to service in amazingly short order. The United States also built and commissioned thousands of other ships, so its fleet eventually dwarfed that of Japan.

For the remainder of the war, the question of why the United States had failed to anticipate and repel the surprise attack on Pearl Harbor was placed mainly on the back burner. In November 1945, however, Congress held hearings on the matter that lasted several months. The final report concluded that Japan was solely responsible for the attack and exonerated most U.S. officials from any wrongdoing. Yet a few scholars and other interested parties continue to doubt this official line. These so-called revisionists charge that the president and others knew of the impending attack, or at least considered it likely, but did nothing to stop it in order to give the country a reason for entering World War II. Though six decades have passed since the attack, it remains one of the most controversial incidents in American history.

Escape from the Capsized *Oklahoma*

Stephen B. Young

For some American military personnel, the terror of December 7 did not end with the departure of the last wave of Japanese planes. One of the seamen assigned to gun turret no. 4 on the USS *Oklahoma*, Stephen B. Young endured a living nightmare that exemplified the destruction and human tragedy of the Pearl Harbor attack and its aftermath. Young and his fellow gunners tried to man their station, but the ship was hit by five torpedoes and began to capsize. Along with many others, they were trapped inside. To their horror, they discovered that all exits were blocked and for the next twenty-five hours were forced to deal with the steadily rising water, a dwindling air supply, and the fear that the vessel would become their tomb. Fortunately for them, all the while rescuers were working feverishly to cut through the hull and free them. The account that follows comes from Young's suspenseful 1991 book describing the ordeal.

The chaos of burning ships in the harbor above was unknown to those of us who were trapped below in the *Oklahoma*. We had just begun our long ordeal.

When Bob Roberts returned to the trunk space [main corridor in the ship's hull] from his unsuccessful exploration of the nearby compartments, he heard some interesting news. Someone said that a man had disappeared underwater from the trunk and hadn't come back.

Excerpted from *Trapped at Pearl Harbor: Escape from Battleship Oklahoma*, by Stephen B. Young (Annapolis: Naval Institute Press, 1991). Copyright © 1991 by Stephen Bower Young. Reprinted with permission.

Where did he go? It was something to think about. Did he find a way out? Or was he blocked somehow in his attempt to escape—hung up—caught on something? It might be worth a try. Roberts didn't know whether to "blow tubes or draw small stores," as the saying goes on the mess decks.

Clarence Mullaley had been aware in the darkness there that someone had tried to go down the water-filled escape hatch in the trunk. Two, he thought, when the light was flashed briefly around the trunk—a couple of blond-haired guys. It was difficult to say, it was so dark down here, and the occasional use of the battle lantern made it seem that much worse when the light went out. Was one of the them the sailor who had grabbed him up out of harm's way back there in the handling room? Savarese, maybe? But he was dark-haired. In any event, they hadn't come back. Someone said to turn out the light so that the batteries would last longer.

Smothering in the Darkness

It was quiet there in the trunk. San Antonio was a long way away thought Mullaley. He'd almost joined the CCC [Civilian Conservation Corps], but he'd heard [newspaper reporter] Walter Winchell say over the radio that if a young man joined the navy when he was seventeen, he could complete a minority enlistment when he was only twenty-one. So, he'd gone and signed up. In boot camp the cooks had told him to drink all the milk he could from the big vats in the mess hall; he might not get another chance.

Chances didn't look too good right now.

Time drifted by. We sat on the inclined ladder or stretched out as best we could to keep out of the water below us. There was little talk. The water lapped gently against the top coaming of the watertight door leading into the trunk from the handling room.

I spoke up, asking of no one in particular, "What happened to Mr. Rommel? He said he was going to come back for us to let us know what was going on."

"Who knows?" said someone from out of the darkness. "Maybe he couldn't."

Another voice said, "He wouldn't just leave us here like this. Maybe the Japs got him."

"Yeah, he must be dead; he would have told us to abandon ship or something."

"Jesus, why did Rommel send us down below, anyway? We were safer up in the turret. Maybe we could have got out."

"Shit."

"What about the poor guys on the shell deck? And how they screamed? We'll never get out of this Goddamn place," someone said in resignation. "To hell with Rommel."

"Knock it off," someone said. It sounded like Red Aldridge. Didn't he have any ideas except to turn off the light or stop talking? He was the senior petty officer present, after all.

But no one as yet would speak of what we all felt, that we might very well die here, deep inside the ship. No one spoke about this because it would do no good.

It was eerie there, hearing the voices of unseen faces speaking out of the darkness of that watery tomb. Yet there was no panic. Only the oppressing resignation to what seemed like almost certain death.

The Oklahoma *began to capsize almost immediately after being hit, trapping many of its crew inside the upturned hull.*

Through it all, despite the apparent hopelessness of our situation, there ran a ray of hope, nothing that anyone could acknowledge as yet. Still, it was there—an undefinable something that told us to hang on—all was not lost.

We were still alive. That subconscious spark that wills a person to live, to never give up though all seems hopeless, was there in that place in varying degrees, depending on the man. Some thought of escape, some of rescue, others were resigned to whatever might be in store for them—even death. Most prayed silently for God to help in whatever way he could. We thought of home, our mothers and fathers, girl friends, or nothing at all.

I could almost feel the dark. The stillness of that deep and stinking place pressed down over us all. I felt I was smothering in the darkness there. Once in a while, a man would cough or move a little, and, every so often, I became aware of the barely perceptible sound of the water as it rose, ever so slowly. . . .

SOS

Suddenly, out of the darkness, a hammering sound . . . in short bursts, then longer . . . automatic.

The noise of it reverberated along the steel decks and bulkheads. It was some distance from us. Where? How far?

Startled out of my semiconscious dreams, I woke instantly, my eyes wide open though I couldn't see. I sat up straight on my bed of peacoats.

What was it? What was that noise? My mind tried desperately to identify it. My heart pounded in my chest. I caught my breath.

It stopped as suddenly as it began. As suddenly, it started again. Had I imagined it? I waited for it to start again. Would it? I strained with the tension of hearing something unexpected.

"What is it?" someone asked off to the left of me.

"Maybe the Japs are trying to torture us," someone replied.

"Yeah, they're letting water in so we can sink all the way," one of the others said.

That didn't make sense at all. "No, no," I said. "It's something else. Listen."

Then . . . the metallic rapping began again. There was no mistaking it. But it was farther away this time. It stopped. We waited. Long minutes went by. Nothing more. More time. It seemed a long time.

What was going on?

Christ Almighty!

Was it possible? Were rescuers looking for us . . . trying to get us out of here? SOS! . . . --- . . . The dog wrench pounded on the bulkhead. We're here! Here in the Lucky Bag [a ship storage compartment]!

Did we dare hope again? We could not speak of it just yet. It was too much.

Why did the hammering stop, then start again, farther away, then stop once more?

My body was rigid with suspense. I dared not hope but I couldn't help it.

More minutes passed. A long time.

Again! The hammering was louder now. Someone spoke the unsaid thoughts of all of us. "They're trying to get to us! To cut us out! They're using an air hammer!"

It was almost too much for us to grasp. To be snatched from almost certain death . . . to live again . . . was more than we were capable of fully understanding just then.

The strain was almost unbearable. My eyes were wide open though I could see nothing; my ears strained for the slightest noise though I could hear nothing for the moment; my mouth was open to breathe in the rancid air my pounding heart demanded.

There it was again! More hammering! Persistent . . . demanding in its urgency. I could feel it as well as hear.

S - O - S! S - O - S! . . . --- . . . banged the dog hammer to let them know where we were.

A sailor began to get excited, panicky, there in the middle of the Lucky Bag, somewhere in the dark. I didn't recognize the voice.

"Get us out! Come get us out of here! God help us!"

It was understandable, but this we didn't need just then. The rest of us realized that to lose control now would help none of us.

"Shut up! Quiet down!" I said to whoever was making the racket.

"I'll bang you over the head with the dog wrench, if you don't stop," someone else threatened.

The sailor got himself in hand and stopped. Despite the suspense, he was the only one to get overly excited—and then just for a few seconds. . . .

The Water Kept Rising

[Eventually they could hear the rescuers directly above them.]

The air hammer rapped its way along the cut in the steel, chipping away at the toughness of the metal; air continued to escape the Lucky Bag in a great hissing sound, and the rushing, splashing noise of the incoming water filled our ears. I looked over at the door and saw water gushing in on either side. In the dim light of the battle lantern, it looked as if the door were bowing inward.

Would the door hold?

"Hurry up, for Christ's sake; the water's coming up to our waists!" a sailor yelled in the lower end of the Lucky Bag.

It was beginning to creep up my feet and legs.

"Keep your heads, fellows. Just do what I tell you. We'll make it!" from the man in charge on the other side of the bulkhead, in Radio IV.

We quieted down.

"Okay, but hurry!" I said. "Some of us are hanging on the overhead."

The chisel at the end of the chipping hammer made its agonizingly slow progress across the top of what would be a rectangular opening a few feet square—just big enough to squeeze through.

Now the hammer began to cut its way down one side of the square. I could see that we would be barely able to fit through the opening. Eleven pairs of eyes urged the chipping hammer along.

The water continued to rise. The door was almost covered. Sailors below me were in water up to their waists and chests now.

It was over my knees and rising.

We edged up higher, up the list of the overhead-deck, hanging on to angle irons and whatever else we could grasp. I hung on with one hand, making room for someone else to come up beside me. I got hold of somebody with my left hand and helped to pull him up out of the water. I don't know who he was.

We were hypnotized, our eyes concentrated on the chipping hammer and its slow progress as it cut its way through the metal. Now it began its third cut, along the bottom of the square.

Hurry! Hurry! Before it's too late. God, the water's coming up higher and higher. Faster. We were as high in the compartment as we could go.

The water was almost up to the level of the bottom cut that the chipping hammer was making. There. Three of the sides were cut through.

"Keep calm; hold on a little longer!" someone said. Julio De Castro, who was talking to us from the next compartment, helped us almost as much by his calm and reassuring manner as he did the pneumatic hammer.

Now the fourth side. The hammer stopped and retreated. Our fingers grasped at the metal to pull it back with our bare hands.

Right now, the difference between life and death was to get that piece of steel bent back so we could get out.

"Look out for your hands, boys. We're going to use a sledge hammer."

So close, yet he was a world away, separated by a quarter of an inch of steel.

The sledge hammer rang against the metal. The three-sided piece of steel bent a little. Again. And again. It just missed Scott's fingers.

"Don't use your hands!"

Gradually, the steel was pushed back; the opening

widened as the water pushed at us from behind. Now the hole was open, just wide enough for us to scrape through!

It was just in time. The water was up to our chests and shoulders, flooding faster and faster into the Lucky Bag.

A Friendly Smile

"Okay! Come on out of there. One at a time. Easy!"

Our friend in the next compartment didn't have to tell us a second time.

Mike Savarese and I were the first two out because of our position next to the bulkhead. I was hanging on to an angle iron just above the hole and when Mike started through, my arm caught him in the throat, "Glug!," and he couldn't move. Not a bottleneck now!

It would have been funny if we weren't so pressed for time.

"Look out, for crissake," Mike choked. "I'm going out."

Anxious as I was to make my own exit, I couldn't keep back a grin. I moved my arm back.

"Come on, Mike, out!" I said.

Savarese ducked through the opening and put a foot down to touch the deck on the other side. He couldn't. So he brought his foot back inside the Lucky Bag and went out with both feet at once this time and hit the deck on the other side. He looked up to see daylight above him.

We urged him on; we weren't out of the woods yet. The flooding waters behind us pushed us forward.

I went out head first without bothering about my feet. Friendly hands on the other side reached out to grab me. Water from the Lucky Bag spilled through the hold as I came out.

I was out! Free! Alive!

I'd made it, after all.

"Up on my back, boy," a big Hawaiian [Navy yard worker Joe Bulgo] grinned. I had never been so glad to see a friendly smile in all my nineteen and a half years.

The Verbal and Official War Declarations

Franklin D. Roosevelt and the U.S. Senate

On December 8, 1941, President Franklin D. Roosevelt addressed a joint session of Congress, giving his solemn, defiant, and now famous declaration of war against the Empire of Japan, reprinted below. Contrary to popular opinion, his words did not make the state of war official, as the U.S. Constitution vests the power to declare war in the Congress. Accordingly, a few minutes after the president gave his address, the legislators met and agreed on the war declaration, as revealed in the official minutes of the Senate, also reproduced below.

President Roosevelt to Congress:

Yesterday, December 7, 1941 a date which will live in infamy the United States of America was suddenly and deliberately attacked by naval and air forces of the Empire of Japan.

The United States was at peace with that nation and, at the solicitation of Japan, was still in conversation with its Government and its Emperor looking toward the maintenance of peace in the Pacific. Indeed, 1 hour after Japanese air squadrons had commenced bombing in Oahu, the Japanese Ambassador to the United States and his colleague delivered to the Secretary of State a formal reply to a recent

Excerpted from "The Address by the President of the United States Declaring War on Japan," and "The Congressional Declaration of a State of War with Japan," *Proceedings of the Senate*, December 8, 1941.

American message. While this reply stated that it seemed useless to continue the existing diplomatic negotiations, it contained no threat or hint of war or armed attack.

It will be recorded that the distance of Hawaii from Japan makes it obvious that the attack was deliberately planned many days or even weeks ago. During the intervening time the Japanese Government has deliberately sought to deceive the United States by false statements and expressions of hope for continued peace.

The attack yesterday on the Hawaiian Islands has caused severe damage to American naval and military forces. Very many American lives have been lost. In addition American ships have been reported torpedoed on the high seas between San Francisco and Honolulu.

Yesterday the Japanese Government also launched an attack against Malaya.

Last night Japanese forces attacked Hong Kong.

Last night Japanese forces attacked Guam.

Last night Japanese forces attacked the Philippine Islands.

Last night the Japanese attacked Wake Island.

This morning the Japanese attacked Midway Island.

Japan has, therefore, undertaken a surprise offensive extending throughout the Pacific area. The facts of yesterday speak for themselves. The people of the United States have already formed their opinions and well understand the implications to the very life and safety of our Nation.

As Commander in Chief of the Army and Navy I have directed that all measures be taken for our defense.

Always will we remember the character of the onslaught against us.

No matter how long it may take us to overcome this premeditated invasion, the American people, in their righteous might, will win through to absolute victory.

I believe I interpret the will of the Congress and of the people when I assert that we will not only defend ourselves to the uttermost but will make very certain that this form of treachery shall never endanger us again.

Hostilities exist. There is no blinking at the fact that our people, our territory, and our interests are in grave danger.

With confidence in our armed forces with the unbounded determination of our people we will gain the inevitable triumph so help us God.

I ask that the Congress declare that since the unprovoked and dastardly attack by Japan on Sunday, December 7, a state of war has existed between the United States and the Japanese Empire.

Proceedings of the U.S. Senate as It Declared War on Japan:

The Senate having returned to its chamber (at 12 o'clock and 47 minutes P.M.), it reassembled and the Vice President resumed the chair.

Mr. BARKLEY. I suggest the absence of a quorum.

The VICE PRESIDENT. The clerk will call the roll. The legislative clerk called the roll.

The VICE PRESIDENT. Eighty-two Senators have answered to their names. A quorum is present.

Mr. CONNALLY. Mr. President, I introduce a joint resolution, and ask for its immediate consideration without reference to a committee.

The VICE PRESIDENT. The joint resolution will be read.

The joint resolution (S.J. Res. 116) declaring that a state of war exists between the Imperial Government of Japan and the Government and the people of the United States, and making provision to prosecute the same, was read the first time by its title, and the second time at length, as follows:

"Whereas the Imperial Government of Japan has committed unprovoked acts of war against the Government and the people of the United States of America:

"Therefore be it Resolved, etc., That the state of war between the United States and the Imperial Government of Japan which has thus been thrust upon the United States is hereby formally declared; and the President is hereby authorized and directed to employ the entire naval and military forces of the United States and the resources of the Government to carry on war against the Imperial Government of Japan; and, to bring the conflict to a successful termination, all of the resources of the country are hereby pledged by the Congress of the United States."

After debate.

The VICE PRESIDENT. The joint resolution having been read three times the question is, Shall it pass?

On that question the yeas and nays have been demanded and ordered. The clerk will call the roll.

The Chief Clerk proceeded to call the roll.

The result was announced: Yeas 82, nays, 0.

So the joint resolution was passed.

Shipping the Wounded Home

Revella Guest

Many of the servicemen and other people wounded in the attack ended up at the largest hospital on Oahu, Tripler Army Hospital, located several miles north of Honolulu and east of Pearl Harbor. Shortly after the second wave of Japanese planes departed on December 7, the injured began to stream into Tripler; and for almost a week the staff of doctors and nurses worked day and night, many unable to find the time even to change their clothes. This account by Lieutenant Revella Guest, a member of the Army Nurses Corps, tells how she and her colleagues coped during these harrowing days and managed, in only a little more than two weeks following the disaster, to begin shipping the injured home to the mainland.

The next morning I was on duty. I went to the dining room, had breakfast, and then went on duty. I was on my ward, ward five, the orthopedic ward. Everything was fine, lazy, not much to do. Some of the patients were out on pass. There were just routine things to do.

All of a sudden the radio started blaring for all military people to report back to their stations. We had porches on the hospital, and I was looking off in the direction of Pearl Harbor from the back porch, and I heard guns and saw smoke, black smoke, coming up. I thought: 'My goodness! I've never seen that before!'

Then the radio started to blare that we were being at-

Excerpted from *Remembering Pearl Harbor: Eyewitness Accounts by U.S. Military Men and Women*, edited by Robert S. La Forte and Ronald E. Marcello (Wilmington, DE: Scholarly Resources, 1991).

tacked by the Japanese. I telephoned down to my friends where they were, and I told them to get up and get dressed because everybody was going to be working, because we were being attacked by the Japanese. Shortly after that, our chief nurse had called down there, and everybody was alerted and on duty.

Since it was the weekend, the staff was more limited with more people having time off. That was like any hospital; you try to get patients in and out before the weekend occurs. Things were just routine. Doctors would come in and make their rounds. If they had somebody there that needed attention, they would be there to give it to him. It was routine. The only things that wouldn't be were emergencies. For routine stuff, if anything came up, then it would wait until Monday morning. That was nothing unusual; it was done that way all the time.

The Lord Was on Our Side

When we got word of the attack, people got back, got on duty, and got things ready. We knew that we were going to have casualties, because we were the largest general hospital on the island. In fact, we were the only general hospital.

First thing I did was to get my ward emptied out of patients that were there. These people were not acutely ill or seriously ill, or ill or anything. We used to call them goldbricks back in those days; you know: 'Go to the hospital so we don't have to do any duty.' Kind of easy. So we got rid of all those fellows. I only had two people left on my ward, who were up in traction. I had to watch those guys like a hawk, because they were going to cut themselves out of traction and go to war.

We didn't know what was going to happen. We didn't know. We were ready, but we didn't know what the assignments of the ward were going to be. At the ward down below, which was ward three, it was emptied out, and they were the preop ward, where patients came in from the emergency room and were put until they could go into the operating room. Then, about 12:00 or 1:00 P.M., my ward was postop.

Every patient that I received had been to surgery. There was no sorting out of patients. You had amputees, abdominal wounds, head injuries. You name it, and it was them.

Most were from the Navy, from Pearl Harbor. By nightfall, about 5:00 in the afternoon, maybe a little later, I know by the next morning, I ended up with sixty-five fresh postoperative patients. We were designed to handle about fifty. We had beds out on porches where we used to put the ambulatory patients. We never put any bedridden patients out there, but they were out there that day. Any place they could get, they were put there.

In postop we had to watch them and see that they were coming out of anesthesia all right. We also had to start IV fluids, but we didn't have the modern equipment that we do today. Our IV bottles were the glass type where you pour the solution in, and you had to be very careful to keep it sterile. I had three of those in my ward, and we went from patient to patient giving them one thousand cc. of fluid. The only thing that we did was be very careful in changing the needle, and then we'd go to the next one to start. We were fortunate, the Lord was on our side, because not one—not one—ever got a chill or infection.

No Time to Change Clothes

That morning only one other nurse was working with me. I often look back and wonder how I did it. How I did it, I don't know. But I did. As they came out of anesthesia, you had to be very careful. You had to watch them and see that they were getting oriented. I never left my own little area; I didn't have time. I couldn't worry about what was happening elsewhere; I didn't have time for it.

In the first place, at night we had no lights. We had a flashlight, and a piece of blue carbon paper was put over the flashlight. That was practically like working in the dark. I can remember going out on the porch and giving a shot to a patient who needed a pain injection. I'd take that carbon paper off, and some guard would holler: 'Put out that light or I'll shoot!' I'd yell: 'Shut up until I give this shot!' It is amazing that more people weren't killed.

I didn't get any relief until four or five days later. I can't remember exactly, because we never thought about time; we had so much to do. I did get back to my barracks to change clothes, get into a clean uniform. That Monday, about 6:00 in the morning, I went to the barracks—no lights. The only light was a blue light in the bathroom. One of the girls had a radio there, and we tried to get some news from the States, but we couldn't. So we gave that up and went back to work.

Fire in the Kitchen

I had an interesting experience. We had one small central supply that was issuing all of our supplies. I thought: 'Well, I'll help them out.' We had other people who came in to volunteer to help, so I had them make bandages and roll them. We had an old gas stove. So I thought: 'Well, I can fill that oven with these things, and, if I can get it filled and keep it on for at least eight to ten hours, then they would be ready for when the day came for the first change of dressings for these patients.' I didn't have any muslin to wrap the supplies in, but we had some brown paper, so we wrapped those in that. I did this. We just had the fire lit, you know. It was an old building.

Pretty soon I was out in the ward doing something, and another nurse came to me and said: 'There is a fire!' I said: 'Where?' She said: 'In the kitchen!' Brother! I went off, and here I am—all my dressings were in flames. I put water in the sink, got a pair of forceps, and was running back and forth taking all my flaming dressings and dumping them into the sink in the water. I thought: 'Wouldn't you know it! All that time and effort gone!' But at least I tried.

I've heard that prostitutes from town came out and volunteered to help at Tripler. I don't believe it. They are not that type of individual. They might have gone somewhere else. I can't say. It makes a good story, but I can't verify it. I don't know.

Later, a friend of mine who had a car—at that time I didn't drive—was working, so she gave me the car keys. I found somebody that could drive, got permission, and I got a gal who wanted me to send a telegram back home. This was about four days afterwards. We went down to the telegraph office, and all we did was sign our names—'Revella.' Some people would have known me by that, and some people who got the telegrams would have wondered who in the world that was, but at least we got telegrams sent off, saying we were safe and sound.

The Highlight of My Career

Another thing we did or didn't do was much charting, because we didn't have the time for it. All we did was put a piece of paper up and tape it to the head of the bed, and we kept track of the last time they'd had any injections. Also, the pharmacy made up a vial of a quarter grain of morphine to use for pain. We carried that in our pockets. We didn't have to record it there, but we just kept it in our pockets so we would save time. All we'd have to do is use it, and, when we were through, we'd get another bottle. Each nurse that was on duty had a vial of that in her pocket and would just go ahead and do it. We just kept track of it at the heads of the beds. We didn't think about charting until about a week afterwards. Then that was a mess, trying to get those records straight, you know.

We got the first shipload of casualties ready to be shipped back to the United States on December 24, 1941. I know that in my ward we were up all night and all day plastering—getting these people in shape for transportation. They sailed for the United States on December 25, 1941.

We didn't have all that modern equipment that they have now, but we did very well with what we had. For a small staff with a big job, it was well done. I was in the military for twenty-five years. I am retired as an Army major. I've had many interesting assignments through my career, but Pearl Harbor was the highlight. It had its tragic moments, and it had its great moments.

Salvaging Damaged Ships

Homer N. Wallin

> In an amazingly short span of time, most of the warships
> damaged in the Japanese raid on Pearl Harbor were salvaged
> and refloated. This immense and costly operation eventually
> came under the direction of Captain (later Vice Admiral)
> Homer N. Wallin, who here describes the basic steps involved
> in salvaging the USS *Oklahoma*, which had capsized during
> the attack. Although the *Oklahoma* never saw action again,
> the salvagers successfully righted and refloated her, providing
> a fascinating textbook example of the tremendous industrial
> resources, as well as recuperative powers, of the United
> States at that time.

Of first importance to Fleet Commanders was the task of
readying ships for a full fleet engagement with the
Fleet of Japan. At that time no information was at hand on
the enemy's location, the strength of his force, or his intentions with regard to landing or seeking a fleet engagement.
The situation which confronted the high command was
therefore to arrive at a priority of work on the various ships,
since those needing a minimum of work should be taken in
hand first and made ready for action.

We have seen from survivors' reports the spirit which per-
vaded our men. Both officers and enlisted were busy saving
the lives of each other and in repelling the enemy. Cow-
ardice was rare if not unknown. Heroism and bravery were

Excerpted from *Pearl Harbor: Why, How, Fleet Salvage, and Final Appraisal*, by Homer
N. Wallin (Washington, DC: Naval History Division, 1968).

the qualities shown by the military. Taking undue risks was commonplace.

The manning of anti-aircraft batteries and the replenishment of ammunition came first. The removal and comfort of the wounded were of almost equal importance. Fighting fires and watertight integrity were the tasks of many. Men were overcome by fumes from the fuel oil which was everywhere, but a shipmate was usually at hand to carry a person to fresh air, or to rescue drowning persons from the water, or from oil and water mixed. Helping shipmates through portholes was the only means of escape still available in certain ships and was responsible for saving many lives.

Step 1: Freeing Trapped Men

As ships capsized, in particular *Oklahoma* and *Utah*, some men were trapped in the ship's lower compartments. They made their presence known by tapping on the structures with wrenches or other tools. These were heard by the men on the hulls of the capsized ships and were answered; the Morse Code was used, and the rescue of the trapped men began. *Oklahoma* showed the maximum promise. The bottom of the ship was all that was visible above water. The ship had capsized through 170 degrees so that its bottom was nearest the surface. By cutting holes through the bottom of the ship the rescue party was able to reach the men who had sought refuge in that part of the ship which was near the open air.

A survivor who had escaped through a hatch at frame 117 stated that men were alive in that locality. At about that time, 0915, Commander Kranzfelder and Lieutenant Mandelkorn from the staff of Commander Battleships, were present, and at 0930 Lieutenant Commander Herbert Pfingstag from the Navy Yard arrived. At first they tried to gain access to the inside of the ship by acetylene torch, using it in locations free of oil and water, but found that the fumes from oil and the cork used for insulation were deadly to the men who were trapped in the locality. Accordingly, they thereafter used compressed air and corresponding tools which were furnished by the Navy Yard and various ships, including

Maryland, Argonne, and *Rigel.* The Navy Yard and ships concerned provided submersible pumps, sound powered telephones, and air ducts for ventilating purposes.

Soon the trapped men were located in the vicinity of frames 131, 116, 78, and 22. The men were all near the bottom of the ship, which at that time was partly visible above the water level of the harbor. It was not until 0800 on 8 December that six men were rescued, and at 1100 eleven more were brought out. Five more were released at 1400 and eight at 1600 on that same date. The last man was not rescued from *Oklahoma* until 0230 on 9 December. All were in good condition except for lack of sleep, food, and sufficient oxygen. Some of the thirty-two men were dependent on an air bubble for sufficient air. Of course the air bubble gradually disappeared and water rose as soon as an opening was made in a compartment. A watch was maintained on the hull of *Oklahoma* until 11 December but no further signs of life were detected.

A great part of the credit goes to the Navy Yard. One of its men showed intrepidity of the highest nature by staying on the job and risking his life as leader until all known survivors had been released from the hull of the ship. He was Julio De Castro, Leadingman Caulker and Chipper, who was awarded a Commendation by the Commandant, Fourteenth Naval District.

Utah lost fifty-eight men in the action. Of those saved one man was rescued through the bottom after the ship had capsized. This was John B. Vaessen, Fireman Second Class, who was later lost. Nearly all of the men who had not been killed or wounded were clear of the lower compartments except Vaessen who remained at his post in the forward distribution room in order to keep lights on the ship as long as possible. He was rescued by helpers from *Raleigh* as well as by a volunteer crew from *Utah* consisting of Machinist S.A. Szymanski, Chief Engineman MacSelwiney, and two seamen. They heard tapping on the bottom and after answering, they cut a hole by acetylene torch, obtained from *Raleigh,* near enough to free Vaessen.

Step 2: Salvage Begins

Rear Admiral William L. Calhoun was in charge of salvage operations by virtue of his position as Commander of the Base Force. He was assisted by officers on his staff, especially Commander Rufus G. Thayer and Commander James H. Rodgers. It happened that Lieutenant Commander Lebbeus Curtis was enroute to the Far East for salvage work and, because of his considerable experience was put in charge as Salvage Engineer. He later was retained in the Base Salvage Organization for several months, at which time he was put in charge of all salvage in the Pacific as Mobile Salvage Engineer. He ultimately was promoted to Rear Admiral.

Considerable progress was made in repairing ships which had only minor damage, especially by furnishing small craft to fight fires and supply pumping equipment. A hero of the times was the lowly garbage lighter, *YG-17*, which had a large pumping capacity. She tied up alongside *West Virginia* to fight her many fires and was successful in her work though beset by Japanese aircraft and continuous strafing. This craft, which won commendations from the Commander of Battleships, had a nostalgic effect on the author because her all-welded sister ship, *YG-16* (often called *Petunia*) was built under his jurisdiction at Mare Island and won a prize of $7500 in 1932 for himself and another officer. *YG-17* which was commanded by Chief Boatswains Mate L.M. Jansen won a well-merited commendation for brave work following the Japanese surprise air raid.

The formal Salvage Organization began on 14 December 1941, an even week after the Japanese attack. It was under the direction of then Commander James M. Steele, who was previously in command of *Utah*. He remained in command of salvage under the Base Force until relieved by the author, Captain Homer N. Wallin, on 9 January 1942. At that time the Salvage Division became a part of the Navy Yard under the Manager, Captain Claude S. Gillette. . . .

Step 3: Righting the Ship

The Japanese planes which passed over the officers' boat landing at Merry Point seemed to concentrate their torpedoes on the battleships which were moored outboard near the northern end of the line. *West Virginia* was hit by as many as seven torpedoes, *Arizona* was sunk at her berth, and *Oklahoma* received from five to seven hits. Early in the onslaught she was put out of action and capsized at her berth.

It was realized that the salvage of this ship would require a combination of the steps taken on *West Virginia* and *Oglala*. The size of *Oklahoma* and her general condition made salvage questionable, although it was deemed important to rid the harbor of a derelict and to make the berth available for other ships. Accordingly, plans were made by the Salvage Division to right her and to refloat her for further disposition.

As early as May 1942 the Navy Department indicated a desire that *Oklahoma* be salvaged. Contractual arrangements were therefore made with the Pacific Bridge Company so that the company could get suitable priorities on required material, and at the same time could hire the right men for the job. A scheme of salvage was therefore drawn up which divided the responsibilities between the Navy and the company. In short, the scheme provided that the ship should first be righted and then floated to a drydock for repairs.

The righting of a ship weighing about 35,000 tons was no easy task. It was accomplished by various means. The important element was, of course, the installation of shore winches on Ford Island. These twenty-one electric winches were anchored in concrete foundations and operated in unison. Each electric winch was capable of about a twenty ton pull through a flexible one-inch wire cable operated through a block system which gave an advantage of seventeen. The three-inch cable, in order to increase the leverage, passed over a wooden strut arrangement which stood on the bottom of the ship about 40 feet high. Then the cable divided into four "cat tails" which were secured to lugs welded to the shell of the ship at frame stations. Calculations indicated that the hull strength was adequate. To assist the twenty-one winches it was at first proposed that submarine salvage pontoons be used on the port side. This was given up because of the difficulty of proper attachment and the presence of mud. The air pressure proposed inside the hull seemed ample.

The air bubble method accounted for almost 20,000 tons of weight initially and was highly effective. It was used on the starboard side after the oil had been removed through the bottom. This totalled about 350,000 gallons of the 1,000,000 gallons originally in the ship. It was placed in oil barges as it was pumped out by three-inch steam reciprocating pumps and air-driven pumps. A steam blanket was used to prevent explosions from oil vapors. This was provided for by having ex-*Navajo* moor alongside and furnish steam and electric power.

The air bubble was divided into five parts to prevent loss of air pressure for the whole ship at a crucial time. The air pressure was about 11–12 pounds, so that the water level was blown down to about twenty-five feet below the surface. This lightened the ship's weight considerably.

There was a large amount of weight in the ship which could have been removed prior to righting or refloating, but difficulty of access made this impracticable. About one-third of the ammunition was taken off but none of the 14-inch projectiles. Some of the machinery was removed from the dry evaporator pump room. The blades of the two propellers were taken off, more to avoid damage to them than to reduce weight.

The above methods assumed that *Oklahoma* would roll instead of slide. Tests, including soil tests, were made to check whether restraining forces should be used to prevent sliding toward Ford Island. It was indicated that the soil of the after two-thirds of the ship facilitated rolling; but the bow section rested in soupy mud which surely permitted sliding. To prevent this about 2200 tons of coral soil were deposited near the bow section, and anchorages along the port side were given up as not necessary.

Consideration was given to some dredging and removal of mud on the starboard side prior to righting, but this was deferred to assure that the vessel would rotate rather than slide. When *Oklahoma* was righted with a list of about fifteen degrees to port the excess soil under the starboard side was washed away by high pressure water jets operated by divers.

During and prior to the righting operation, care was taken that all purchases were equalized. This was accomplished by the use of strain gauges on the hauling wires at each bent or strut. The one-inch flexible cable was speeded up or slowed down to equalize these strain gauges. Observation posts were established on barges to note the effect of righting movements, and especially to note whether the ship was rotating or sliding.

The wooden bents became less effective as their leverage decreased when the ship gradually assumed a position approaching ninety degrees. When the list was about sixty-eight degrees to port the bents or head frames were cast off and floated clear. From then until the ship reached thirty degrees to port the pull was directly on the lugs welded to the port shell. Then the hauling cables were secured to the ship's topsides, especially to strong portions such as barbettes and the starboard crane foundation.

The ship rolled as desired. The stern section traveled a greater distance than the bow section toward the quays. This was because of the greater area of the stern. In any event, the vessel came to rest with a mean draft of 49½ feet at high tide (high tide is something less than 2½ feet above mean low water). The list to port was only 2 degrees and 10 minutes. The behavior of the ship was in strict accord with the models which were constructed and tested before salvage operations were begun. *Oklahoma* was right side up by 16 June 1943, the work having started 8 March 1943.

Step 4: Floating the Ship

When *Oklahoma* was nearly upright, divers investigated the damage on her port side. They found that the port side was pretty well opened up from torpedo explosions which oc-

curred before and during capsizing. They cut away struc-
tural wreckage and took necessary measurements for temporary patches. The topside damage was apparent; contact
with the bottom had broken off the masts and most other superstructure.

The divers found that a large patch was required from
frames 43 to 75. This patch was 130 feet long and 57½ feet
high as it extended well under the turn of the bilge. In addition, several patches were installed, usually of wood and
sealed with Tremie underwater concrete. For instance, one
went between frames 31 and 43, another between frames 74
and 96.

The large patch was in five parts and was primarily steel
and wood. It was sealed by underwater concrete at the ends
as well as at the bottom. The sections were made watertight
by puddings between the sections. Again, underwater concrete was essential. In all over 1000 tons of concrete were
poured. Hook bolts were used by the divers in drawing up
the patches to the hull of the ship.

The main deck aft was underwater, but not enough to prevent refloating. However, in order to increase the waterplane
area and in order to improve the stability during refloating
a wooden cofferdam like *Oglala* and *California* cofferdams
was installed from frames 85 to 115.

In the meantime the divers were busy jetting out mud,
closing drains and sanitary outlets, cutting sluicing holes,
closing watertight doors and hatches, etc. In due time they
followed the reduction of the water level and closed off the
main leaks in the hull and the patches.

During the last period of righting the weight of the ship
was reduced by about 3500 tons through using the buoyancy
forward of frame 30 and aft of frame 115. This was done
primarily by deep-well pumps which quickly removed the
water in those areas.

Then 10 ten-inch deep-well pumps augmented by lesser
pumps were more than enough to lower the water level in
the ship, but by this time the Navy Yard was in possession
of twelve-inch pumps, both electric and diesel. In the main

patch eighteen and twenty-inch electric pumps were used at a later date. As in other ships, the water level was reduced according to schedule which permitted adequate testing for toxic gases, plenty of ventilation and lighting, and removal of the 400 or more human bodies which were in *Oklahoma.*

In order to insure positive stability, some ballasting by sea water was scheduled in the machinery spaces. Great care was exercised by the Salvage Superintendent to insure that the ship would come afloat with a minimum of list. Actually she came afloat on 3 November 1943 with a mean draft of about forty-six feet and a starboard list of twenty-six minutes. The list was increased to about one degree to starboard and so maintained by pumping water from the port engine room to the starboard engine room. The hauling tackles were removed after the ship came afloat and the various leaks were well in hand.

Thought was given to the damage caused by teredo worms on patches after long submergence. This was found to be negligible, as was the teredo damage to the teak decking of the ship.

For the purpose of refloating very little weight was removed. However, prior to drydocking, attention was given to this important consideration. It was not practicable to remove stores, but anchors, chain, remaining oil, and so on were taken ashore. Mud in the ship was jetted to electric pumps by water jets in the hands of divers.

Oklahoma's Final Fate

The ship was placed in Drydock Number Two on 28 December 1943 with a mean draft of thirty-six and a half feet and a list to starboard of nearly three degrees. The list was purposely put on the vessel in order to favor the port side and its patches. In order not to lose buoyancy the introduction of water to attain the desired list was not permitted; instead four submarine salvage pontoons, each having a lift capacity of eighty tons, were used on the outside of the main patch.

The total draft of *Oklahoma* was nearly thirty-nine feet because the main patch extended several feet below the keel.

During the trip to the drydock the electric-driven pumps were replaced by diesel-driven. The list was taken off in drydock and the ship settled on the blocks provided without undue incident. The pontoons were removed, and the patches were likewise taken off to expose the damage which the ship had sustained. A strict fire watch was maintained on board.

The Navy Yard employees were quick to start with temporary repairs. They worked from inboard to obtain watertightness of the hull inasmuch as the drydock was available for emergency dockings of damaged major ships of the fleet. Thus the drydock had to be vacated on seventy-two hours notice. However, no emergency developed, and *Oklahoma* remained there for several months. During her time at the Navy Yard she was stripped of guns and some of the auxiliary machinery. The ship was unloaded of ammunition and stores. She was decommissioned on 1 September 1944 and sold for scrap for $46,000 on 5 December 1946 to the Moore Drydock Company. On 10 May 1947 she left Pearl Harbor under tow of two tugs but was lost in a storm at sea about 500 miles northeast of Hawaii on 17 May 1947.

Congress's Investigation of the Attack

U.S. Congress

> An event as large-scale, devastating, and embarrassing as the
> Pearl Harbor attack naturally raised many questions by Ameri-
> can legislators and ordinary citizens alike. How was it possible
> for such a disaster to take place? And who should be held
> responsible? From November 15, 1945, to May 31, 1946,
> Congress held hearings with the official title of the Joint Con-
> gressional Committee on the Investigation of the Pearl Harbor
> Attack. A detailed report was issued afterward. The general
> conclusion of the majority on the committee, summarized
> below, was that the attack was entirely unprovoked and that
> the blame lay solely with the Japanese leadership. Further-
> more, the U.S. president and his advisers had done everything
> they could to avoid war. The committee found that army and
> navy intelligence had been lax and that the War Department
> should have kept the Pacific forces on a higher state of alert. A
> small minority of officials and scholars disagreed and some do
> so to this day. In what has come to be called the revisionist
> view, Roosevelt and his advisers supposedly knew about the
> impending attack but allowed it to happen so that the United
> States would have a concrete reason for entering World War II.

Conclusions with Respect to Responsibilities

1. The December 7, 1941, attack on Pearl Harbor was an unprovoked act of aggression by the Empire of Japan. The

Excerpted from *Report of the Joint Committee on the Investigation of the Pearl Harbor
Attack* (Washington, DC: U.S. Government Printing Office, 1946).

treacherous attack was planned and launched while Japanese ambassadors, instructed with characteristic duplicity, were carrying on the pretense of negotiations with the Government of the United States with a view to an amicable settlement of differences in the Pacific.

2. The ultimate responsibility for the attack and its results rests upon Japan, an attack that was well planned and skillfully executed. Contributing to the effectiveness of the attack was a powerful striking force, much more powerful than it had been thought the Japanese were able to employ in a single tactical venture at such distance and under such circumstances.

3. The diplomatic policies and actions of the United States provided no justifiable provocation whatever for the attack by Japan on this Nation. The Secretary of State fully informed both the War and Navy Departments of diplomatic developments and, in a timely and forceful manner, clearly pointed out to these Departments that relations between the United States and Japan had passed beyond the stage of diplomacy and were in the hands of the military.

4. The committee has found no evidence to support the charges, made before and during the hearings, that the President, the Secretary of State, the Secretary of War, or the Secretary of Navy tricked, provoked, incited, cajoled, or coerced Japan into attacking this Nation in order that a declaration of war might be more easily obtained from the Congress. On the contrary, all evidence conclusively points to the fact that they discharged their responsibilities with distinction, ability, and foresight and in keeping with the highest traditions of our fundamental foreign policy.

5. The President, the Secretary of State, and high Government officials made every possible effort, without sacrificing our national honor and endangering our security, to avert war with Japan.

6. The disaster of Pearl Harbor was the failure, with attendant increase in personnel and material losses, of the Army and the Navy to institute measures designed to detect an approaching hostile force, to effect a state of readiness

commensurate with the realization that war was at hand, and to employ every facility at their command in repelling the Japanese.

7. Virtually everyone was surprised that Japan struck the Fleet at Pearl Harbor at the time that she did. Yet officers, both in Washington and Hawaii, were fully conscious of the danger from air attack; they realized this form of attack on Pearl Harbor by Japan was at least a possibility; and they were adequately informed of the imminence of war.

8. Specifically, the Hawaiian commands failed—

(a) To discharge their responsibilities in the light of the warnings received from Washington, other information possessed by them, and the principle of command by mutual cooperation.

(b) To integrate and coordinate their facilities for defense and to alert properly the Army and Navy establishments in Hawaii, particularly in the light of the warnings and intelligence available to them during the period November 27 to December 7, 1941.

(c) To effect liaison on a basis designed to acquaint each of them with the operations of the other, which was necessary to their joint security, and to exchange fully all significant intelligence.

(d) To maintain a more effective reconnaissance within the limits of their equipment.

(e) To effect a state of readiness throughout the Army and Navy establishments designed to meet all possible attacks.

(f) To employ the facilities, matériel, and personnel at their command, which were adequate at least to have greatly minimized the effects of the attack, in repelling the Japanese raiders.

(g) To appreciate the significance of intelligence and other information available to them.

9. The errors made by the Hawaiian commands were errors of judgment and not derelictions of duty.

10. The War Plans Division of the War Department failed to discharge its direct responsibility to advise the com-

manding general he had not properly alerted the Hawaiian Department when the latter, pursuant to instructions, had reported action taken in a message that was not satisfactorily responsive to the original directive.

11. The Intelligence and War Plans Divisions of the War and Navy Departments failed:

> (a) To give careful and thoughtful consideration to the intercepted messages from Tokyo to Honolulu of September 24, November 15, and November 20 (the harbor berthing plan and related dispatches) and to raise a question as to their significance. Since they indicated a particular interest in the Pacific Fleet's base this intelligence should have been appreciated and supplied

The Revisionist View

Noted scholar John Toland is one of the leading modern revisionists regarding the Pearl Harbor attack. Here, from his Infamy: Pearl Harbor and Its Aftermath, *he suggests that President Roosevelt thought the attack would ultimately benefit the United States; the Japanese would do little damage to the "impregnable" defenses in Hawaii, and Japan's failure would eliminate it as a threat in the Pacific.*

This course was a calculated risk but Roosevelt, like Churchill, could take a gamble. Nor did risk at that moment seem so great. [A] memorandum the President had received . . . in May 1941 [described] Oahu as the strongest fortress in the world, with assurances that any enemy naval task force would be destroyed before it neared Pearl Harbor. Long a Navy man, Roosevelt believed in its power. Also he had been receiving reports on the low efficiency of Japanese pilots, whose planes were second rate. Consequently the Pacific Fleet would not only stem any Japanese attack with little loss to U.S. shipping but deal a crushing blow to *Kido Butai* [the Japanese naval strike force] itself. One of the keenest admirals in the Navy, "Terrible" Turner, believing this, had told the Navy Court of Inquiry, "I knew our carriers were out, and with the warnings which had been given, the Hawaiian commanders for their assistance, along with other information available to them, in making their estimate of the situation.

(b) To be properly on the *qui vive* to receive the "one o'clock" intercept and to recognize in the message the fact that some Japanese military action would very possibly occur somewhere at 1 P.M., December 7. If properly appreciated, this intelligence should have suggested a dispatch to all Pacific outpost commanders supplying this information, as General Marshall attempted to do immediately upon seeing it.

12. Notwithstanding the fact that there were officers on twenty-four hour watch, the Committee believes that under

---

I felt we would give them a pretty bad beating before they got home by our shore-based aircraft and by our carriers."

Such a defeat would have been catastrophic to the Japanese militarists and perhaps eliminated Japan as a menace in the Pacific with a single blow. Moreover, [Admiral] Kimmel's two available carriers would be out of Pearl Harbor and those warships left were in no real danger of being sunk. Aerial bombs were not that much of a threat and the waters of Pearl Harbor were too shallow for a torpedo attack. . . .

Despite shortcomings, Franklin Delano Roosevelt was a remarkable leader. Following the maxim of world leaders, he was convinced that the ends justified the means and so truth was suppressed. . . .

A small group of men, revered and held to be most honorable by millions, had convinced themselves it was necessary to act dishonorably for the good of their nation—and incited the war that Japan had tried to avoid. . . .

The mistakes and cruel acts of violence committed by both Japan and America must not be forgotten—only understood. Enemies in the past, and friends today, they must remain equal partners in the future.

John Toland, *Infamy: Pearl Harbor and Its Aftermath.* Garden City, NY: Doubleday, 1982, pp. 318–19, 324.

all of the evidence the War and Navy Departments were not sufficiently alerted on December 6 and 7, 1941, in view of the imminence of war.

Recommendations

Based on the evidence in the Committee's record, the following recommendations are respectfully submitted:

That immediate action be taken to insure that unity of command is imposed at all military and naval outposts.

That there be a complete integration of Army and Navy intelligence agencies in order to avoid the pitfalls of divided responsibility which experience has made so abundantly apparent; that upon effecting a unified intelligence, officers be selected for intelligence work who possess the background, penchant, and capacity for such work; and that they be maintained in the work for an extended period of time in order that they may become steeped in the ramifications and refinements of their field and employ this reservoir of knowledge in evaluating material received. The assignment of an officer having an aptitude for such work should not impede his progress nor affect his promotions. Efficient intelligence services are just as essential in time of peace as in war, and this branch of our armed services must always be accorded the important role which it deserves.

That effective steps be taken to insure that statutory or other restrictions do not operate to the benefit of an enemy or other forces inimical to the Nation's security and to the handicap of our own intelligence agencies. With this in mind, the Congress should give serious study to, among other things, the Communications Act of 1934; to suspension in proper instances of the statute of limitations during war (it was impossible during the war to prosecute violations relating to the "Magic" without giving the secret to the enemy); to legislation designed to prevent unauthorized sketching, photographing, and mapping of military and naval reservations in peacetime; and to legislation fully protecting the security of classified matter.

That the activities of Col. Theodore Wyman, Jr., while

district engineer in the Hawaiian Department, as developed by the Army Pearl Harbor Board, be investigated by an appropriate committee of the Senate or the House of Representatives.

That the military and naval branches of our Government give serious consideration to the 25 supervisory, administrative, and organizational principles hereafter set forth.

Chronology

1853

A U.S. naval squadron commanded by Commodore Matthew Perry coerces the Japanese, much against their will, to begin trading with Western nations, initiating Japan's long-standing resentment of the West.

1868

Japan, a feudal society, begins an incredible transformation that turns it into a major industrial/military power almost overnight.

1904–1905

Testing its new power, Japan fights and defeats Russia.

1922

In an international treaty, the United States and its allies further anger Japan by limiting the number of large warships it can build.

1931

As part of a growing effort to build an empire in the Far East, Japan invades the Chinese province of Manchuria.

1941

January 7: Admiral Isoroku Yamamato writes to Japan's war minister, advocating a surprise attack on the U.S. Pacific fleet stationed at Pearl Harbor on the island of Oahu, Hawaii.

November 26: The U.S. State Department sends a ten-part message to the Japanese government urging a peaceful resolution of the two countries' differences. There is no immediate answer. That same day, a Japanese naval strike force leaves Japan bound for Hawaii.

December 5: The FBI records a telephone call in which a Japanese woman living on Oahu sends coded information about American military installations to a source in Japan. That same day, the Japanese strike force reaches its rendezvous point near Hawaii and receives the order to proceed with the attack on Oahu.

December 6: The Japanese government finally delivers its answer to the American message of November 26; Japan says it is fed up with U.S. policies in the Far East and will no longer negotiate with the United States.

December 7
6:00 A.M.: The Japanese fleet, now situated about 230 miles north of Oahu, launches its first wave of warplanes.

7:02: A U.S. Army radar operator sees unidentified planes approaching Oahu.

7:53: Mitsuo Fuchida, lead pilot of the Japanese air attack force, flies over Pearl Harbor and sees the American ships lined up like sitting ducks.

7:55: The first bombs fall on Ford Island (in the center of the harbor), Wheeler Field, and Hickam Field; hundreds of U.S. planes are destroyed on the ground.

8:10: A 1,760-pound bomb smashes into the USS *Arizona*, which is enveloped in a huge fireball and sinks in only nine minutes.

8:12: The USS *Utah* capsizes.

8:50: The USS *Nevada* manages to get underway but is attacked on its way out of the harbor; the captain grounds the ship to avoid being sunk in the harbor entrance.

8:54: A second wave of Japanese planes damages the USS *Pennsylvania*, *Cassin*, and *Downes*.

10:00: The second wave of planes departs, leaving Pearl Harbor, Hickam Field, Wheeler Field, and several other military installations in ruins and 2,343 people dead.

December 8: President Franklin D. Roosevelt stands before a joint session of Congress and delivers a stirring declaration of war against Japan. At Pearl Harbor, trapped sailors continue to be rescued from the capsized ships.

December 25: The first contingent of wounded servicemen begins the long trip home from Oahu.

1942
On June 4, the United States delivers Japan a crushing defeat at Midway, west of Hawaii, marking the beginning of a relentless offensive that drives the enemy back toward its home islands.

1945
On September 2, Japan surrenders to the United States and other Allies aboard the USS *Missouri* in Tokyo Bay. On November 15, Congress launches hearings into the causes and culprits of the Pearl Harbor attack.

1946
On May 31, Congress concludes its hearings. Soon afterward it issues a report saying that the sole responsibility for the attack on Hawaii rests with Japan.

For Further Research

Leatrice R. Arakaki and John R. Kuborn, *7 December 1941: The Air Force Story.* Hickam Air Force Base, HI: Pacific Air Forces Office of History, 1991.

Bruce Blevin Jr., *From Pearl Harbor to Okinawa: The War in the Pacific, 1941–1945.* New York: Random House, 1960.

Winston Churchill, *The Second World War.* 6 vols. New York: Bantam Books, 1962.

Richard Collier, *The Road to Pearl Harbor: 1941.* New York: Atheneum, 1941.

John Costello, *The Pacific War.* New York: Rawson, Wade, 1981.

James F. Dunnigan and Albert A. Nofi, *Victory at Sea: World War II in the Pacific.* New York: William Morrow, 1995.

Mitsuo Fuchida and Masatake Okumiya, *Midway: The Battle That Doomed Japan.* Annapolis: Naval Institute Press, 1955.

Donald M. Goldstein and Katherine V. Dillon, eds., *The Pearl Harbor Papers: Inside the Japanese Plans.* New York: Brassey's, 1993.

A.A. Hoehling, *The Week Before Pearl Harbor.* New York: Norton, 1963.

Edwin P. Hoyt, *Japan's War: The Great Pacific Conflict, 1853–1952.* New York: McGraw-Hill, 1986.

Joy W. Jasper et al., *The USS Arizona.* New York: St. Martin's Press, 2001.

Robert S. La Forte and Ronald E. Marcello, eds., *Remembering Pearl Harbor: Eyewitness Accounts by U.S. Military Men and Women.* Wilmington, DE: Scholarly Resources, 1991.

Edwin T. Layton, *"And I Was There": Pearl Harbor and Midway—Breaking the Secrets.* New York: William Morrow, 1985.

Walter Lord, *Day of Infamy.* 1957. Reprint, New York: Henry Holt, 2001.

Milton W. Meyer, *Japan: A Concise History.* Lanham, MD: Rowman and Littlefield, 1993.

Walter Millis, *This Is Pearl! The United States and Japan: 1941.* New York: William Morrow, 1947.

Samuel E. Morison, *Oxford History of the American People.* New York: Oxford University Press, 1965.

———, *The Rising Sun in the Pacific, 1931–April 1942.* Boston: Little, Brown, 1968.

Gordon W. Prange, *At Dawn We Slept: The Untold Story of Pearl Harbor.* New York: McGraw-Hill, 1981.

———, *God's Samurai: Lead Pilot at Pearl Harbor.* New York: Brassey's, 1990.

Edwin O. Reischauer, *Japan: The Story of a Nation.* New York: Knopf, 1970.

Report of the Joint Committee on the Investigation of the Pearl Harbor Attack. Washington, DC: U.S. Government Printing Office, 1946.

Kazuo Sakamaki, *I Attacked Pearl Harbor.* New York: Association Press, 1949.

Peter J. Shepherd, *Three Days to Pearl: Incredible Encounter on the Eve of War.* Annapolis: Naval Institute Press, 2000.

Louis L. Snyder, *The War: A Concise History, 1939–1945.* New York: Dell, 1960.

Ronald H. Spector, *Eagle Against the Sun: The American War with Japan.* New York: Free Press, 1985.

John Toland, *Infamy: Pearl Harbor and Its Aftermath.* Garden City, NY: Doubleday, 1982.

————, *The Rising Sun: The Decline and Fall of the Japanese Empire, 1936–1945*. New York: Random House, 1970.

Paul J. Travers, *Eyewitness to Infamy: An Oral History of Pearl Harbor, December 7, 1941*. New York: Madison, 1991.

Homer N. Wallin, *Pearl Harbor: Why, How, Fleet Salvage, and Final Appraisal*. Washington, DC: Naval History Division, 1968.

Stanley Weintraub, *Long Day's Journey into War: December 7, 1941*. New York: Dutton, 1991.

H.P. Willmott, *Pearl Harbor*. London: Cassell, 2001.

Stephen B. Young, *Trapped at Pearl Harbor: Escape from Battleship Oklahoma*. Annapolis: Naval Institute Press, 1991.

Index

Allies, 30
Antares (supply ship), 89–90
Arakaki, Leatrice R., 26, 130
Argonne (submarine tender), 89,
 90, 91–92
Arizona (battleship), 18
 attack on, 23–24, 81, 83, 84,
  97–99
 damage to, 84
Australia, 30

Barrett, Joe, 120, 121
battleships. *See individual names
 of ships;* warships
Bellows Field, 18–19, 26
Bicknell, George W., 60
Blick, Roy, 137
Bolan, George, 122
Bratton, Rufus, 20, 21
Brunson, Clyde W., 134, 135

Calhoun, William L., 164
California (battleship), 18
 attack on, 24–25, 84, 100–106
Canada, 30
Carson, Carl, 97
Cassin (destroyer), 27, 81, 87
China
 Japanese control of land in, 15
 Japanese-U.S. negotiations on,
  67–68, 70–71
 U.S. intentions on, 73–75
Churchill, Winston S., 29
Colorado (battleship), 18
Crosley, Paul, 84
Curtis, Lebbeus, 164

Downes (destroyer), 27, 81

Enterprise (carrier), 18, 31
Erickson, Ruth, 133
Ewa Marine Corps Air Station,
 19, 26

feudalism, 14–15, 18
Ford Island, 22
Formosa, 15
Fort Kamehameha, 137–40
Fourteen Part Message, 64, 67–75
France, 30
Fuchida, Mitsuo, 18, 76
 describing Pearl Harbor attack,
  24, 94, 95
 satisfaction with Pearl Harbor
  achievement and, 27–28
 training for torpedo runs and,
  44, 45

Genda, Minoru, 34, 41, 44, 45
Ginger, 116
Great Britain
 Japanese attacks on bases of, 29
 Japanese grievances against,
  67–68
 warnings about Pearl Harbor to
  agent from, 34, 50–59
Greece, 30
Grew, Joseph, 20
Guam, 29, 153
Guest, Revella, 156

Helena (light cruiser), 91
Helm (destroyer), 85
Hickam Field
 destruction at, 25–26
 eyewitness account of attack on,
  116–19, 120–24

location of, 18–19
targets at, 114
Holmes, Ephraim P., 110
Hong Kong, 29, 153
hospitals, 133–36, 157

Indochina, 15–16, 65–67, 73

Japan
  civilian response to Pearl
    Harbor attack by, 28
  grievances against the United
    States by, 72–75
  long-standing contempt for
    America by, 13–16
  mistakes and miscalculations
    by, 30–31
  negotiating efforts by, 67–69,
    70–72
  proposal to United States by,
    69–70
  as responsible for Pearl Harbor,
    171–72
  Roosevelt's letter to emperor of,
    65–67
  U.S. declaration of war against,
    29–30, 154–55
Japanese military
  aircraft, 21–22
  description of Pearl Harbor
    attack by pilot, 94, 95
  fleet of, 16–17, 44–45
  in Indochina, 15–16, 65–67
  operational planning for Pearl
    Harbor by, 38–40, 41–42
    follow-up, 44–48
    route attack, 46–47, 48–49
  preparations for Pearl Harbor
    by, 76–79
  training, 37–38
  war preparations by, 36–37

Kaga (carrier), 47
Kaneohe Naval Station, 19, 26

Kenworth, Jesse, 24
Kidd, Isaac C., 24
Kimmel, Husband E.
  learning of Pearl Harbor attack,
    23, 83
  shot at while witnessing attack,
    86
  warnings about Pearl Harbor
    and, 20
Kita, Nagao, 45
Koran, Flora Belle, 125
Koran, Stephen, 125, 130
Korea, 15

Layton, Edwin T., 22–23, 82
Lexington (carrier), 18, 31
Lord, Walter, 44, 45

Malaya, 29, 153
Manchuria, 15
Maryland (battleship), 18, 111
  attack on, 24–25, 83
McGoran, John H., 100
Midway Island, 153
Mikawa, Gunichi, 17
military. *See* Japanese military;
  U.S. military
Monaghan (destroyer), 22, 87
Mori, Motokazu, 60
Mullaley, Clarence, 145

Nagumo, Chuichi, 16
Nevada (battleship), 84, 87, 91,
  96
New Zealand, 30
nurses, 133–36, 156–60

Oglala (mine layer), 91
Oklahoma (battleship), 18
  attack on, 24, 81, 83, 84, 90
  crew trapped in capsized,
    144–51, 162–63
  salvaging, 165–70
Olsen, Vernon, 93

Ono, Kenjiro, 17–18

Pearl Harbor attack
on airfields, 25–26, 86, 114–15
counterattack at Wheeler
Field, 128–30
eyewitness account at Hickam
Field, 116–19, 120–24
photographing damage from,
130–32
as told by Japanese pilot, 79
on Battleship Row, 21–25
eyewitness accounts of, 81,
82–86, 90–91, 93–96
seamen's personal account of,
97–99, 100–106, 107–109
second wave of, 87
as told by Japanese pilot, 94,
95
defending Oahu coast during,
138–40
as epic historical event, 13
events leading up to, 34
ignored warnings on, 20–21, 34
to British agent, 50–59
congressional report on,
174–75
tapped phone conversation by
FBI and, 60–63
Japanese concerns and fears on,
17–18
Japanese plans for, 16–17
Japanese response to, 28
Japanese responsibility for,
171–72
on living quarters, 125–28
medical efforts to help victims
of, 133–36, 156–60
second wave of, 26–27, 110–12
as a surprise, 34–35
controversy over, 142–43
revisionist explanation of, 174,
175
time line of, 81

U.S. failure to detect, 172–74
U.S. response to, 28–29, 87–88,
152–55
Pennsylvania (battleship), 27, 81,
87
Perry, Matthew, 14
Pesek, Joseph A., 120
Philippine Islands, 153

Raleigh (light cruiser), 81
Roberts, Bob, 144, 145
Rodgers, James H., 164
Roosevelt, Franklin D.
declaration of war by, 29,
154–55
knowledge of Pearl Harbor
attack by, 174, 175
letter to emperor of Japan by,
64–67
reaction to Pearl Harbor attack
by, 29, 142, 152–54
response to Japan in Indochina
by, 16
Russia, 15
Ryan, Joseph, 89

sailors. *See* servicemen
servicemen
casualties, 26, 28
caught in second wave of
attacks, 110–12
escaping from burning ships,
24–25
freeing trapped men in ships,
162–63
heroic efforts by, 26, 161–62
medical help for, 133–36, 142,
156–60
personal account by Pearl
Harbor survivors, 97–99,
100–106, 107–109
rescuing soldiers after attack,
91–92
shipping wounded home, 160

trapped in capsized ship, 144–51
Shaw (destoyer), 27, 81, 87
Shepherd, Peter J., 20–21, 34, 50
Shiga, Yoshio, 44
ships. *See individual names of ships;* warships
Singapore, 29
Solace (hospital ship), 96
Southern, Ira, 25, 26
Spector, Ronald H., 21
Steedly, Bill, 25, 107
St. Louis (light cruiser), 105–106

Taiwan, 15
Tennessee (battleship), 24–25
Thayer, Rufus G., 164
Tojo, Hideki, 28
Toland, John, 174, 175
Tyler, Kermit, 21–22

United States
  declaration of war against Japan by, 29–30, 154–55
  epic historical events in, 13
  immediate reaction of, to Pearl Harbor attack, 87–88
  Japan's proposal to, 69–70
  Japanese grievances against, 72–75
  Japanese underestimation of, 31
  Japan's negotiating efforts with, 67–69, 70–72
  long-standing Japanese contempt for, 13–16
  radio strikers, 89–90
  response to Pearl Harbor attack in, 28–29
U.S. Congress, 171
U.S. military
  congressional recommendations on, 176–77

enlisting in, 137–38
failure to detect Pearl Harbor attack, 172–74
as unprepared, 19–20
warnings ignored by, 20–21
see also Pearl Harbor attack; servicemen; warships
Utah (battleship), 96, 81, 163

Vaessen, John B., 163
Van Valkenburgh, Franklin, 24
Vestal (repair ship), 108
Vietnam, 15–16

Wake Island, 29, 153
Wallin, Homer N., 161
warships
  limits on number of, 15
  located at Pearl Harbor, 18–19
  salvaging, 142, 164–70
  see also names of individual ships
West Virginia (battleship), 18, 24, 83, 84, 165
Wheeler, Burton K., 28
Wheeler Field, 18–19, 26
  counterattack at, 128–30
  destruction at, 114
  personal account of attack at, 130
  photographing damage from, 130–32
Williams, John A., 84
Willmott, H.P., 13
Wyman, Theodore, Jr., 176–77

Yamamoto, Isoroku, 17, 34, 36
YG-17 (garbage lighter), 164
Young, Cassin C., 109
Young, Stephen B., 144
Yugoslavia, 30

About the Editor

Historian and award-winning author Don Nardo has written or edited many books for young adults about American wars, including *The Mexican-American War*, *The War of 1812*, *The Indian Wars*, and surveys of the weapons and tactics of the American Revolution, Civil War, and Persian Gulf War. Mr. Nardo lives with his wife, Christine, in Massachusetts.